Liberalism in Neoliberal Times

Liberalism in Neoliberal Times

Dimensions, Contradictions, Limits

Edited by Alejandro Abraham-Hamanoiel, Des Freedman,
Gholam Khiabany, Kate Nash, and Julian Petley

Goldsmiths
Press

© 2017 Goldsmiths Press
Published in 2017 by Goldsmiths Press
Goldsmiths, University of London, New Cross
London SE14 6NW

Printed and bound in the United States of America.
Distribution by The MIT Press
Cambridge, Massachusetts, and London, England

A CIP record for this book is available from the British Library

ISBN 978-1-906897-40-6 (hbk)
ISBN 978-1-906897-45-1 (ebk)

www.gold.ac.uk/goldsmiths-press

Goldsmiths
UNIVERSITY OF LONDON

Contents

1

Introduction

Gholam Khiabany

Raymond Williams once suggested that the term 'liberal has, at first sight, so clear a political meaning that some of its further associations are puzzling.' This, as Williams demonstrated, is partly because the word itself has a long and fascinating history that dates back to the fourteenth century. The original uses of 'liberal' were mostly positive. *Liberal* was a mark of distinction, a free man in contradistinction with those who were not; *liberal arts* was a reference to skills appropriate for men who had means and status; *liberal* also came to be defined as generous, open-minded, and unorthodox. The distinction, from its very first usage, was all about class, privilege, and status. However, 'liberal' also had, and still retains, negative meanings. For example, cultural and social conservatives still associate 'liberal' with unrestrained and undisciplined attitudes and behaviour. *Taking liberties* is pejorative, as is a liberal reading/attitude to facts and figures.[1]

In the realm of politics the term is just as complex and puzzling. On the one hand, being liberal has been regarded as being open-minded, progressive or even radical, while, on the other hand, liberals are attacked for either being insufficiently radical (from the Left) or being too progressive (such as in the United States). The prevailing definition of liberalism (as an ideology, political philosophy, and tradition) has historically revolved around tolerance, progress, humanitarianism, objectivity, respect for and promotion of reason, democracy, and human rights. To be considered a 'liberal' (in this sense) can still be seen as a positive thing. Yet despite receiving a very good press throughout its history, liberalism has also been subject to passionate and sustained critiques by the Left and the illiberal. For the latter, liberalism has gone too far; for the former, it has never gone far enough. Raymond Williams, for example, argues that liberalism, while referring to a 'mixture of liberating and limiting ideas', is 'essentially, a doctrine of possessive individualism' and that it is, therefore, 'in fundamental conflict not only with socialist but with most strictly social theories.'[2]

In the opening chapter of this collection, William Davies argues that the basic premise of liberal thought is the equality of individuals before the law—a conception that stresses the negative immunity of citizens from political intervention and coercion. Yet, as Davies notes, private property 'has long been recognised as a fundamental individual right within liberal frameworks, which partly accounts for the connection between political and economic liberalism.' Historically, however, economic participation and entitlement have been limited to a small minority of people with resources and capital. It was precisely this liberation of men to 'own property' that Marx criticised so trenchantly. 'None of the so-called rights of man,' Marx argued in *On the Jewish Question*, 'therefore, go beyond egoistic man, beyond man as a member of civil society—that is, an individual withdrawn into himself, into the confines of his private interests and private caprice, and separated from the community.'[3]

The variety of uses and connotations certainly makes sweeping generalisation about liberals and liberalism impossible. Yet the seed of contradictions was visible from the very first moment of liberalism: the strength of liberalism—its commitment to emancipation—is also its main weakness in that there were at least three major exclusion clauses in this project. Not only love for liberty but also contempt for people of the colonies, the working class, and women more generally were factors that united liberal thinkers. In his book on liberalism, Domenico Losurdo reminds us that liberal thinkers—including Locke, Smith, and Franklin—shared an enthusiasm for 'a process of systematic expropriation and practical genocide first of the Irish and then of the Indians', as well as for 'black enslavement and the black slave trade'.[4] The contradictions at the heart of liberalism are sharply expressed in its approach to 'liberty'. Losurdo stresses that slavery was not something that preceded liberalism but rather fostered its maximum development after the success of liberal revolutions. The total slave population in the Americas increased from 330,000 in 1700 to 3 million in 1800 and then to over 6 million in the 1850s. The tangle of emancipation and enslavement also shows itself in the slogan of the rebel colonists during the American War of Independence: 'We won't be their Negroes'.[5]

Even for the most radical of liberal thinkers, John Stuart Mill, democracy was fit only for a 'civilised' community. 'Despotism', Mill asserted, 'is a legitimate mode of government in dealing with barbarians, provided the end be their improvement, and the means justified by actually effecting that end.'[6] Indeed, the 1789 'Declaration of the Rights of Man' said nothing about the rights of slaves, the people of the colonies, or women. And the power of capital in the land of 'barbarians' came not through 'peaceful competition' (as is usually claimed) but through the barrel of a gun.

The scars are still deep and still fresh. Slavery continued by other means in both the colonies and in the metropolis. The ideology of superiority and difference that underpins this barbarism is liberal in its origin and in its make-up. Contemporary versions of this thinking about freedom and democracy—as evidenced through recent 'humanitarian interventions'—continue to evince a sense of superiority in which liberals enforce 'democracy' upon the 'less enlightened'. The love of freedom and liberty that is central to the idea of liberalism is indeed one that, in its realisation, has all too often been easily sacrificed at the altar of the interests of capital and (imperial) states.

Liberty, for Mill as well as other liberals, was exclusive to those with 'developed' faculties. As such, it was not just the 'barbarians' but also the native working class, the illiterates (that is, the majority) that were considered ineligible for the right to vote. Nothing was considered worse than giving representation (and the right to vote) to the working class for it would give them the chance to negotiate for better wages and working conditions. The lack of freedom in the colonies, therefore, was extended to the metropolis and issues of race and class intertwined from the start.

In short, while liberty has provided an ideological bulwark against authoritarianism, it has also always been connected to the configurations of the liberal democratic capitalist state. Linked to this, therefore, is another contradiction: the equation of liberalism with democracy. Italian philosopher and political scientist Norberto Bobbio,[7] who was on a (peaceful) mission to bring liberalism and the Left closer together, argues that a 'liberal state is not necessarily democratic'. Indeed, while liberalism is about 'a particular conception of the state', democracy 'denotes one of the many possible modes of government'.[8] Bobbio further suggests that the relationship between liberalism and democracy resolves itself into a more problematic relation between liberty and equality. The question, contrary to rigid liberal thought, has not been simply about liberty or freedom, but about the precise nature and definition of liberty itself: freedom from what and to do what?

Much of the history of liberalism has been about separating these two historic demands for liberty and equality. Throughout the history of modern times, and even in the most liberal of societies, what has been lacking is precisely the more expansive, anti-authoritarian sense of 'liberal'. The United States is a significant example. The decision to invade Iraq, revelations about extraordinary renditions, and the surveillance of key members of the UN and major US allies have also shown the rule of law to be selective, if not a myth. At times in which even the liberalism of liberal America has been tested to its limits after the terrorist attack of 9/11, and in the period in which the much celebrated First Amendment has been hijacked variously by corporate America, the gun lobby, and the Ku Klux Klan, and with visible and increased state tyranny and violence against African Americans, rarely has the United States been so desperately in need of a touch of anti-authoritarian liberalism.

As William Davies explains in some detail in the opening chapter, the relationship between economic and legal liberalism and the market fundamentalism advocated by neoliberals is another contradictory and contested arena today. If neoliberalism is a political project at least as much as it is an economic theory, ideologically it is associated with a classically minimal liberal state, with the efficiency of 'free markets' as against the ponderous and wasteful outcome of state-planned economies and nationalised industries that characterised Keynesian welfare states. In practice, however, neoliberalism has been linked with increasingly authoritarian uses of state power—at home and abroad—and with re-regulation of the economy to protect financial capital rather than the deregulation championed by advocates of neoliberalism. What we have witnessed is not the withdrawal of the state as such but further interventions by the state and the redistribution of wealth in favour of capital. We have only to consider here the 'bail out' of banks that were 'too big to fail' following the financial crisis of 2008, and the violent repression of protests against 'austerity measures' demanded by 'global markets' (more or less personified in the European Union and the IMF) that we continue to see played out in Greece.

And here lies a further contradiction. What has been considered as a beautiful dimension of liberalism, both in its longevity and its attachment to a basic welfare provision, is the social democratic experiment in Europe after World War II and the use of large-scale public spending to enact progressive social and economic measures. Yet this has been the exception rather than the norm in the history of capitalism and, even here, it has taken place because of the pressure of mass movements and social struggles. Similarly, the struggles for democracy in the colonies and the metropolis came from outside liberalism. India became free not because of liberalism but in fierce opposition to it. The struggle for liberation and modernization also came as part of broader struggle for independence. The right to vote, welfare reforms, and public services were gained through organised working-class movements in the metropolis. It was not liberals but emerging radical movements that made those gains after forcing the liberals to retreat from their positions that saw the law of the market as the 'divine' law.

Yet liberalism continues to be a live question for radical movements for equality and freedom today whether in relation to imperialism, gender, race, or austerity. Liberals and liberalism remain, therefore, very relevant in contemporary neoliberal circumstances as sources of ideas and action. This book aims to provoke critical engagement with the theories, histories, practices, and contradictions of liberalism today, in particular by taking specific contemporary topics such as education, social justice, media, and race and gender equality as a way of assessing the transformations in, as well as the transformative aspects of, liberalism. Contributors to this volume reflect on how liberalism—in all its forms—continues to underpin specific institutions such as the university and the 'free press' and how these ideas about liberalism are mobilised in areas such as human rights, minority rights, and liberal political cultures.

In the opening chapter, William Davies highlights important distinctions between political liberalism, economic liberalism, and neoliberalism and pays particular attention to the clash between liberalism and neoliberalism. He outlines and explains key terms that are mobilised through the rest of the volume. The subsequent chapters in the collection are organised into four sections. The first is focused on human rights. Putting 'liberalism' and 'human rights' together tends to prompt critique from political theorists. Liberalism is invoked to justify injustices that are simultaneously made invisible: the oppression of women, colonial adventures, socio-economic inequalities, disciplining disruptive subjectivities. If human rights are too closely tied to liberalism, justice becomes impossible. As Ratna

Kapur, paraphrasing Gayatri Spivak puts it, while human rights 'appear to be something we cannot not want', their progressive potential is limited through too close association with liberalism. While many contributions argue that we should remain suspicious of liberal claims, others—for example Başak Çalı, writing on the European Court of Human Rights and Roberto Gargarella, writing on the Argentinian Constitution—make a case for the continuing value of political liberalism in relation to human rights. Monika Krause refuses the link between liberalism and human rights altogether: in a pragmatic sense, perhaps what guides thought and practice on human rights is more concrete examples than ideology?

The second section deals with liberalism and the media. Alejandro Abraham-Hamanoiel explains how media monopolies confine freedom of expression in South America, while Colin Leys discusses the failure of the British media, and particularly the BBC, to explain the implications of the 2012 Health and Social Care Act. Des Freedman critiques 'muscular' liberal reactions to the *Charlie Hebdo* killings and John Steel stresses the importance of moving beyond traditional liberal conceptions of the role of the media in society which, he argues, are lacking in critical rigour and are too firmly embedded in outmoded conceptions of democracy. Jonathan Hardy, taking the example of the UK's Channel 5, demonstrates that neoliberalism infuses modern communications companies not simply in the manner in which they are owned and structured but also in the kind of content that they habitually produce—a situation that will not be changed simply by swapping corporate owners from time to time. Finally Robert McChesney invokes Alexander Meiklejohn and his 1948 work, *Free Speech and Its Relation to Self-Government*, to argue that the actually existing capitalist model for the media has been an abject failure in democratic terms. He argues that a commitment to liberal values also requires a commitment to the establishment of an independent, largely non-commercial media sector, and that any measures to protect freedom of expression, such as the First Amendment in the United States, need to be conceived primarily as policy prescriptions for a self-governing society and not as protective legislation for investors in the communication industries. In the concluding chapter of this section, Natalie Fenton examines mass surveillance by governments on citizens and suggests that if 'freedom of assembly and protest are one of the basic tenets of liberalism, it is hard to surmise anything other than in neoliberal times, we have reached the very end of its limits.'

Contributors to this section disagree about the extent to which 'classic' social-liberal values are relevant to the analysis of media in a neoliberal age, but they are clearly united in their belief in the need for such analysis and critique and in their dismissal of the notion that the marketplace of ideas can flourish only if the media are left to regulate themselves. Nor are they persuaded that 'old' problems will be remedied by the new media: networked communications may have transformed the capacity for messages to be created and exchanged, yet problems of access and control remain as pertinent as ever. Meanwhile issues such as privacy take on ever greater salience, as both state and corporate interests increasingly monitor people's online lives, demonstrating the way in which the state—for all its protestations about the importance of 'deregulation'—and the market can become fatefully intertwined, to the detriment of the citizen.

The next section explores the idea of the liberal university. Universities, as Joan Pedro-Carañana points out, are key

Enlightenment institutions—predicated on a belief that the pursuit of knowledge might be an end in itself with tremendous benefits to humanity, creativity, and economy. Enlightened passions, however, appear to have been drowned out in recent years by the icy calculation of a bottom line that has little time for immeasurable principles like tolerance, equality, and universalism. According to John Holmwood, 'universities no longer function to ameliorate social status and inequality, but are part of the new status order of a renewed patrimonial capitalism.' Liberal values concerning the intrinsic desirability of knowledge and its contribution to shared dialogue have been repackaged so that universities tend to function, both in their administration and their output, as service providers to the highest bidders and most lucrative customers.

Articles in this section highlight the failure of liberalism to resist this trend and point to the implantation of a neoliberal logic in the restructuring of higher education across the world. Contributors address the complicity of academics in their own downfall (Michael Bailey), the commercialisation of social science research (John Holmwood), the virtual disappearance of the liberal arts in a marketised education system (Toby Miller), the twisting of liberal principles of free speech to undermine minority voices (Howard Littler), the incorporation of universities into a security state (Jonathan Rosenhead), as well as the inability of traditions of academic freedom to protect radical voices, like that of Steven Salaita, from persecution by university leaders (Priyamvada Gopal). The university, it appears, has lost its way—its status as a key pillar of a liberal society has been undermined by the instrumental logic of contemporary neoliberalism—and it needs extensive re-imagining and rebuilding if it is ever to rediscover a role of critical enquiry and truly original thinking.

The particularism that undermines the apparently universal claims of liberalism is most visible in relation to two other 'isms': sexism and racism. These provide the focus for the final section of the collection. Here, the major exclusion clauses that are at the heart of this system of knowledge have been shaped and defined by the very paradox of its own universality. As Arun Kundnani points out: 'In the abstract, there is no reason why liberal principles of individual freedom cannot be applied consistently. And principled liberals have been essential to many struggles against racism and imperialism. But, liberalism is not just a body of ideas; it is also a social force. And, as such, there are structural reasons why liberalism keeps undermining its own ideals.' While this is a theme that runs through the entire collection, it is especially highlighted in this section.

Annabelle Sreberny, for example, introduces two additional terms that she believes are crucial to the liberal tradition: the people and the public. These, she argues, have come under renewed attack in neoliberal times. However, in her discussion of cultural and political rights and identities, she also states that the gap between the idea and the reality of a supposedly homogeneous 'we' is getting ever larger. Milly Williamson reminds us that liberal thought was not aligned with 'female emancipation' or 'gender equality' and yet, in recent times, women's emancipation has been used as a justification for illegal wars. This issue is further explored in Deepa Kumar's assessment of colonial feminism. Other contributions in this section tackle the polarising topics of anti-Muslim racism and Zionism. Kundnani refutes the binary division of liberalism versus Islam and suggests that it is not the integration of some people in the system but the system itself that is the problem. Haim Bresheeth then traces the history of Zionism as a liberal ideology and its replacement with a militaristic and racist state.

The starting assumption of this project was that the emancipatory potential of liberalism is far too important to be left to self-proclaimed liberals. We hope that the thirty-seven articles in this collection will confirm the value of this perspective.

Notes

1. Raymond Williams, *Keywords: A Vocabulary of Culture and Society* (London: Fourth Estate, 2014).
2. Ibid, 179–80.
3. Karl Marx, "On the Jewish Question," in *The Marx-Engels Reader*, ed. Robert C. Tucker (New York: Norton, 1978), 43.
4. Domenico Losurdo, *Liberalism: A Counter History*, trans. Gregory Elliott (London: Verso, 2011), 20.
5. John Adams, quoted in Losurdo, *Liberalism*, 49.
6. John Stuart Mill, Mill, *On Liberty* (New York: Cosimo, 2005), 14.
7. For a critique of Bobbio's views see Perry Anderson, *Spectrum* (London: Verso, 2005).
8. Norberto Bobbio, *Liberalism and Democracy* (London: Verso, 1990), 7.

2

What Is 'Neo' about Neoliberalism?

William Davies

In the buildup to the 2015 General Election, Nigel Farage, leader of the UK Independence Party (UKIP), reiterated his support for an 'Australian-style points system' as a means of controlling immigration, the policy issue that his party had prioritised above all others. What was curious about Farage's statement was not the policy commitment itself, which had been known for some time, but the liberal rhetoric that he used to justify it. Writing in *The Daily Telegraph*, Farage argued 'what Ukip wants is not to do down migrants. It's not to stigmatise, or discourage, or blame people for coming to this country and trying to make a better life for themselves' and that the 'points system' is the only *fair* basis for managing immigration.[1]

At first sight, this is a simple case of rhetorical triangulation: the party that is known to be least favourable towards immigration can afford to speak in liberal tones, giving a compassionate veneer to anti-immigrant politics. But the priority attached to the 'points system' suggests that there was something more substantial at work here. UKIP's liberal rhetoric is grounded firmly in the alleged fairness of the 'points' methodology itself. As the party's website reported, the 'Australian-style points system' upholds a 'principle of equal application to all people'.[2] What could be more liberal than that?

At the core of this policy debate is the schism between 'liberalism' and 'neoliberalism' as two rival philosophies or 'rationalities' of politics.[3] The notion of an immigration 'points system' assumes that the question of legitimate migration is ultimately an economic one of granting citizenship only to certain economic categories of migrant. And yet many economic liberals would argue that borders should simply be relaxed across the board, so as to promote greater labour market flexibility in general. Clearly, UKIP are not seeking *that*.

A 'points system' works through allocating different scores to each prospective citizen, based on their qualifications, linguistic ability, and work experience. A certain number of points are then required to gain entry. The purpose of such a system is therefore to discriminate between rival migrants, which is precisely how it resonates with the politics of UKIP. Where racial or cultural prejudices may focus on arbitrary signifiers, the promise of the 'points system' is to calculate different human capabilities according to the economistic metaphor of human capital, a concept that originated in the work of Chicago School economist Gary Becker in the 1960s.

For reasons that I will explore, the 'points system' can be seen as exemplary of neoliberal government in action, and highlights a number of critical distinctions between political liberalism, economic liberalism, and neoliberalism. These three philosophies or rationalities each has its own distinctive historical and intellectual genesis, and the three survive alongside each other today, sometimes complementing one another, sometimes clashing. But it is possible and helpful to make out some of the critical terms of their differentiation, so as to get a clearer sense of how liberalism and neoliberalism conflict.

Understood in a political sense, liberalism is a philosophy that treats individuals as the bearers of certain rights recognised within a system of sovereign law. Most crucially, they have the right to life and the necessities that go with that, which includes certain economic necessities. Property has long been recognised as a fundamental individual right within liberal frameworks, which partly accounts for the connection between political and economic liberalism. A crucial premise of all liberal thought and politics is that individuals all possess an equal status as legal subjects, regardless of other inequalities and differences that might divide them. Often (but not necessarily) this is complemented with a philosophy of equal democratic citizenship.

To a great extent, it is the liberal commitment to legality and equality before the law that provokes a party such as UKIP in the first place. The sense that judges are able to overrule democratically elected governments, upholding human rights charters that treat all cultures and nations equally, has been one of the key drivers of reactionary politics in the West since the 1960s. In the United States, the role of the Supreme Court in legalising abortion was one of the main catalysts for the 'culture wars' that revived conservatism and fundamentalism in the 1980s. In its dream of an overarching architecture for society and resort to metaphysical language of 'rights', it always runs the risk of seeming inflexible, unscientific, and 'out of touch'.

Of course, a national polity can seek to withdraw from international agreements and laws, so as to reduce the scope of their political liberalism to national subjects only. Yet still this form of political liberalism upsets those communitarians who wish to see collective life governed by tradition and identity, rather than abstract legal codes. In the absence of dictators or oligarchies to mobilise against, the risk with political liberalism is that it becomes an increasingly niche type of special interest, a preoccupation for lawyers, human rights activists, and members of Liberty.

The fact that political liberals share an agenda with economic liberals is therefore one of the most crucial resources for the authority of the former. Economic liberals start from the utilitarian premise that unregulated market exchanges are welfare-enhancing, the claim at the heart of Adam Smith's inauguration of economic science. This translates into the political programme known as 'laissez-faire', in which the state provides minimal forms of legal regulation and protection, such as property rights, contract law, and some collective goods such as national defence, but otherwise allows markets to regulate themselves. Historically speaking, the high point of this political programme was the British economy of circa 1820–1870.

What is crucial for laissez-faire to be realised is the idea that political and economic realms (corresponding broadly to state and market) exist virtually independently of one another. Someone can be a full citizen in a political sense, but impoverished in an economic sense. States can punish criminals or wage war, but they should not interfere with market relations between private actors. And so on. This ideal of separate political and economic realms has been widely criticised, not only by Marxists on the grounds that it provides a cover for class exploitation (liberating the proletariat merely to alienate themselves), but notably also by Karl Polanyi, who argued that it was only ever an illusion.[4] From Polanyi's perspective, the state is never entirely absent from the economic realm, but is constantly at work in manufacturing and enforcing the economic freedoms that proponents of laissez-faire treat as 'natural'.

It is relatively easy to imagine a migration policy forged around the principles of economic liberalism, indeed Tony Blair's government was briefly willing to defend rising migration levels on grounds of aggregate welfare-enhancement in the years preceding 9/11.[5] But again, the sense that the market will all just sort it out, while the government stands back, is provocative to anyone who believes that markets need designing, constructing, and manipulating towards the greatest local advantage. This includes populists such as UKIP—but it also includes neoliberals.

The term 'neoliberalism' refers to various things, but is perhaps best understood with reference to an intellectual and political movement that sought to reinvent liberalism in a twentieth century capitalist context. This context differed from that of Victorian liberalism in various ways, but especially in terms of the scale of bureaucratic centralisation in both business and government. Intellectually it began in the 1930s,[6] gathered momentum via think tanks and academic exchange in the post-war period,[7] and then attained a grip on governments and multilateral institutions from the 1970s onwards.[8] The contrast between this 'neo' liberalism and its political and economic forebears can best be understood in terms of three distinctions.

Firstly, neoliberalism has never pursued a weaker state; indeed it is a political philosophy and policy agenda that has always looked to the state to reshape society around its ideals. As Michel Foucault went to great lengths to stress, it is *not* another form of laissez-faire and, instead, grants the state a key role in shaping how economic freedom is to be defined and instantiated.[9] So, in the case of immigration, the liberal notion that economic welfare will be maximised by simply throwing open the national labour market to all-comers would be resisted from a neoliberal perspective. It is entirely plausible, from a neoliberal perspective, that the state *might* seek to regulate something like labour flows, to serve certain strategic economic goals.

Belief in a strong state is not in itself a contradiction of older traditions of *political* liberalism. Thomas Hobbes's foundation of liberal political philosophy made the state a precondition of freedom, requiring untold reserves of centralised power in order to sustain a civil society. Neoliberals typically work within this more pessimistic tradition of liberal philosophy, and share the same idea of the absolutist state as offering the a priori framework for freedom. The liberals they are most suspicious of are the more egalitarian, optimistic ones, who view markets and civil society as spaces of potential self-rule and self-regulation.

Secondly, neoliberalism abandons the liberal conceit of a separation between political and economic realms of life. Ultimately, everything can be treated in economic terms, including state, law, democracy, leadership, and civil society. Political ideals and values are treated as dangerous and liable to result in tyranny. It is far safer, from a neoliberal perspective, to view all spheres of human conduct as economic and to remodel political or cultural spaces around the example of the market.

This doesn't necessarily equate to full privatisation of public goods. Quasi-privatisation can occur via the introduction of pseudo-markets: education, health, the arts, and so on become evaluated, ranked, and governed 'as if' they were operating in a fully-functioning market. This is viewed as preferable to judging and governing them on their own terms, which are deemed liable to lead to corruption and self-serving behaviour. Ultimately, political institutions of law, tradition, and sovereignty are viewed as nonsense from a neoliberal perspective.[10] Questions of citizenship and justice (which shape questions of migration for political liberals) would be simply ignored within a neoliberal framework, and replaced with technocratic questions of productivity, incentives, risk, and return on investment. The 'points system' is a product of this technocratic sidestepping of sovereign concerns.

Thirdly, neoliberalism treats competition as the crucial and most valuable feature of capitalism.[11] There is a simple reason for this: through processes of competition, it becomes possible to discern who and what is valuable. As Friedrich Hayek argued, competition is a 'discovery process'.[12] In the absence of well-organised competition, there is either a single myopic viewpoint imposed by intellectuals and planners (the problem of socialism); or there is a relativist cacophony of voices, all seeking to drown each other out (the problem of democracy). But this raises the urgency of competitions being well-planned and administered, hence the power of auditors, rankings, ratings, coaches, motivational techniques, and sporting metaphors in contemporary culture.

For economic and political liberals such as Smith, the great merit of the market was that it brought people together. It produced a new form of equality, whereby people would trade with each other as equals, and sympathise with the viewpoints of one another. Ultimately, exchange would produce social peace.[13] For neoliberals, things are very different. Capitalism's central property is not integration but discrimination: competition separates the leader from the follower; the winner from the loser; the striver from the skiver: the dynamic, productive,

English-speaking migrant from the benefit scrounger. Anything that the state can do to support this sorting process (such as reform of the education system) is deemed welcome. At a macro scale, nations themselves must strive to distinguish themselves from one another, like corporations or brands pursuing divergent strategies towards 'competitiveness' in the 'global race'.[14]

There is a political and economic logic to this, and not merely a reactionary impulse. Indeed, there is still some vestige of liberalism here, but it is deeply buried. The assumption underlying the neoliberal worldview is a sociological one, namely that we live under conditions of modernity, where the fabric of human existence is constantly being remade. The question is whether we want to privilege political and collective institutions in that dynamic, or economic and individualistic ones. The contention of neoliberals is that the latter is a safer basis for liberalism than the former, even if it means living in the shadow of corporate oligopolies and in a culture of constant entrepreneurship that tips eventually into depressive narcissism.

What, then, is left of 'liberalism' under 'neoliberal' conditions? Can the language of fairness really be seized so easily by UKIP? The notion that fairness now consists in an evaluative, discriminating methodology 'applied equally to all people' offers a reasonably accurate depiction of the weak normativity of neoliberalism. This is scarcely recognisable as liberalism.

One thing that the neoliberal pioneers possessed that contemporary liberals might take heed of, however, was an ethos of *redesign and innovation*. Rather than just look to the market or the law to uphold their ideals, as economic and political liberals respectively have done, neoliberals saw the need for active reinvention of both. New policy instruments would be needed to build a new liberalism for the twentieth century, some of which have now found their way into the hands of conservatives and reactionaries such as Farage. The question is whether another reinvention is possible today, based on a different liberal imagination from that which privileges only economics and competitiveness, extended to every walk of life.

Notes

1. Nigel Farage, "Ukip's Immigration Policy is Built on Fairness," *Daily Telegraph*, March 3, 2015.

2. UKIP, "UKIP Launches Immigration Policy," accessed February 23, 2016, http://www.ukip.org/ukip_launches_immigration_policy.

3. Michel Foucault, *The Birth of Biopolitics: Lectures at the College de France, 1978–79* (Basingstoke, UK: Palgrave Macmillan, 2008); Wendy Brown, *Undoing the Demos: Neoliberalism's Stealth Revolution* (New York: Zone Books, 2015).

4. Karl Polanyi, *The Great Transformation: The Political and Economic Origins of Our Time* (Boston: Beacon Press, 1957).

5. For example, Stephen Glover et al., *Migration: An Economic and Social Analysis. RDS Occasional Paper No 67* (London: Home Office, 2001).

6. Angus Burgin, *The Great Persuasion: Reinventing Free Markets Since the Depression.* (Cambridge, MA: Harvard University Press, 2012).

7. Philip Mirowski and Dieter Plehwe, eds., *The Road from Mont Pèlerin: The Making of the Neoliberal Thought Collective* (Cambridge, MA: Harvard University Press, 2009).

8. David Harvey, *A Brief History of Neoliberalism* (Oxford: Oxford University Press, 2005).

9. Foucault, *Birth of Biopolitics.*

10. William Davies, "Economics and the 'Nonsense' of Law: The Case of the Chicago Antitrust Revolution," *Economy and Society* 39, no. 1, (2010): 64–83. doi:10.1080/03085140903020655.

11. Foucault, *Birth of Biopolitics*; Pierre Dardot, *The New Way of the World: On Neoliberal Society*, trans. Christian Laval (London: Verso, 2014); William Davies, *The Limits of Neoliberalism: Authority, Sovereignty and the Logic of Competition* (London: Sage, 2014).

12. Friedrich Hayek, "Competition as a Discovery Procedure," *Quarterly Journal of Austrian Economics* 5, no. 3, (2002): 9–23.

13. Albert Hirschman, *The Passions and the Interests: Political Arguments for Capitalism Before Its Triumph* (Princeton, NJ: Princeton University Press, 1977).

14. Philip Cerny, *The Changing Architecture of Politics: Structure, Agency, and the Future of the State* (London: Sage, 1990).

I

Liberalism and Human Rights

What is the relationship between human rights and liberalism? For many on the Left, they are synonymous. The relationship is less clear-cut, however, if we consider that international law on human rights includes social and economic rights alongside the civil and political rights privileged in the West. This section of the book brings together provocative articles by authors from across the world to consider the relationship between liberalism and human rights in a number of very different contexts.

Some chapters propose a critique of human rights as exclusionary of groups whose members do not conform to the white, male, middle-class archetype of the liberal individual. They map how liberalism's blind spots are being reproduced in contemporary rhetoric concerning human rights. In other cases, authors reflect on the extent to which human rights fall far short of liberalism; where, for example, constitutions that reflect international human rights norms legally support state repression. In addition, there are further challenges to the view that debates on human rights are nothing but liberalism dressed up for the twenty-first century—especially when we consider movements that aim to realise economic as well as social rights. In such cases, human rights start to take on more of a socialist than a liberal edge. Rather than taking for granted that we always already know what they are in relation to liberalism, the section aims to convey a sense of the pluralism and diversity of human rights and of the political contexts in which they are invoked today.

3

Human Rights, Markets, States, and Movements

Kate Nash

Marx's critique of human rights as classically liberal in 'On the Jewish Question' is well-known.[1] In this polemic essay Marx compares human rights (chiefly the right to liberty and security) to political rights. While human rights protect individual property in civil society, the political rights of citizens prescribe a 'heaven on earth' of cooperation and self-determination in the state. Natural law ideals of human rights encoded in positive law work against state socialism for Marx (and of course this is not his political aim, which is 'human emancipation'). Marx was writing about the 'Rights of Man and of the Citizen' of the French Revolution. Is his critique still relevant today?

In contrast to eighteenth-century 'rights of man', international human rights today are more social democratic than liberal. The Universal Declaration of Human Rights (on which subsequent UN Conventions of human rights elaborate) was made in the wake of the New Deal in the United States, alongside the creation of welfare states in Europe, and with the input of delegates from the USSR. Far from prescribing a state that polices the security of private property, the post-war international human rights regime looks more like a blueprint for social democracy. The same goes, though more obliquely, for European human rights law today, at least as far as ending discrimination goes. It is true that the European Convention on Human Rights of the Council of Europe is limited to civil and political rights—to classically liberal rights of freedom from the state, and also to democratic rights to elect and be elected that actually alter classical liberalism. But in the European Union, these are now supplemented with social rights in the Lisbon Treaty and in the case law of the European Court of Justice. Constitutions in other parts of the world—in India and Latin America—go still further, adding multicultural group rights as well as social and economic rights. On paper, if human rights are liberal, they are a version of liberalism that is more collectivist than individualist (more 'New Liberal' than classical liberalism).

But perhaps if human rights are social democratic on paper, in principle, they may be liberal in practice. Indeed, there is a good deal of suspicion today that human rights are *neoliberal* in practice.

There is certainly some basis to these suspicions. It is effectively in the gap between international law and compliance with that law that human rights become part of projects of neoliberal imperialism. It is a paradox that in international law it is only states that violate human rights, but it is also only states that have the responsibility to guarantee human rights. It is a paradox, but it is not nonsense. Making states the guarantors of human rights against themselves involves another presupposition: that states are all basically the same. It presupposes that states have all been through the same historical formation: that they have developed administrative capacities that depersonalise and limit power through bureaucracy and the separation of powers; and that they have been made relatively responsive to an active civil society of non-governmental organizations and investigative journalists. In other words, making states the guarantors of human rights presupposes states that are both liberal and democratic.

At best this presupposition rests on a very partial and idealised history of state formation in the Northwest—the European settler states that share broad commonalities in terms of capitalist industrialisation and the development of citizens' rights. And what they also share is a centrality to twentieth-century geopolitics. Because what this history leaves out most significantly is the history of colonialism. As Partha Chatterjee has argued, in most of the world people live in postcolonial states.[2] Postcolonial states were formed in the nineteenth century to be administered from elsewhere, so they were never as intense or as uniform in relation to citizens as colonial states: they were built on obedience to local powers and subjection rather than on winning consent. In this respect, human rights can be seen as a continuation of imperialism: they are largely irrelevant to most people in most of the world, and they serve chiefly as justifications for international public policies, even military interventions that are led by Northwestern states. And neoimperialism is connected to neoliberalism in that at the same time they are engaged in 'leading' human rights internationally, Northwestern states are themselves being restructured by regulation designed to free markets from social welfare settlements, which were achieved through democratisation, to the advantage of global elites.

This understanding of human rights is in many ways compelling. But it is not the whole picture. It is complicated by

constructions of human rights against public policies that promote markets. I'll just give a couple of the most interesting recent examples here. One is the human rights to health claimed
by Treatment Action Campaign in South Africa, which took on
drug manufacturers to bring down the price of retroviral drugs
and put in place a national network of grassroots health care for
people suffering from AIDS.[3] Another example is the Rights of
Peasants demanded by La Vía Campesina, which is linked to
MST (the Movement for Workers without Land) that squats
large landholdings in Brazil.[4] Both these mobilisations invoke
human rights as political ideals, they use the law, and they address states at local, national, and international scales, but they
do not depend on the law or on the administrative capacities of
the states in which they are situated. In fact, both have operated
on the border between legality and illegality in order to exercise rights in practice. Both participate in paradoxes of human
rights, between citizenship and humanity, universalism and diversity, emancipation and governance.[5]

It seems that whether you think human rights are liberal
depends in large part on where you look, what you are looking for, and how. Hannah Arendt is often invoked in discussions of human rights—both for and against. For Arendt what
is important is not the state or the law but political community.
Famously, she sees rights as guaranteed only where there is a
'right to rights'.[6] This is an enigmatic phrase—which is surely
part of its attraction. What seems clear, though, is that investi-
gating what 'the right to rights' might look like in practice today
will surely lead us in directions that neither classic liberals nor
Karl Marx would ever have imagined.

Notes

1. Karl Marx, "On the Jewish Question," in *Early Writings* (London: Penguin, 1992).
2. Partha Chatterjee, *The Politics of the Governed: Reflections on Popular Politics in Most of the World* (New York: Columbia University Press, 2004).
3. William Forbath et al., "Cultural Transformation, Deep Institutional Reform and ESR Practice: South Africa's Treatment Action Campaign," in *Stones of Hope: How African Activists Reclaim Human Rights to Challenge Global Poverty*, eds. Lucie E. White and Jeremy Perelman (Stanford, CA: Stanford University Press, 2011).
4. María Elena Martínez-Torres and Peter Rosset, "La Vía Campesina: The Birth and Evolution of a Transnational Social Movement," *Journal of Peasant Studies* 37, no.1 (2010): 149–75. doi:10.1080/03066150903498804.
5. Kate Nash, *The Political Sociology of Human Rights* (Cambridge: Cambridge University Press, 2015).
6. Hannah Arendt, *Origins of Totalitarianism* (New York: Harcourt Brace, 1968).

4

Human Rights: From Universalism to Pragmatism

David Chandler

Kate Nash makes the useful point that universalist claims for human rights have historically been articulated within very different forms of rights- and needs-based understandings. For example, there is a great deal of difference between human rights claims articulated in the form of natural rights, in order to oppose state regulation and interference in the social sphere, and human rights claims articulated in the form of social democratic demands for state provision of services and support. Of course, human rights claims can be made to enable the expansion of state regulatory power as much as for the retreat of the state and can be articulated in pre-modern, liberal, and neoliberal forms. In short, discussing human rights in the abstract, or in 'for or against' terminology, is rarely a useful or productive exercise.

Many commentators have observed the fact that universalist claims of promoting human rights have become an integral part of a new, more hierarchical international order, undermining UN Charter restrictions on the use of military force and justifying new, more coercive forms of international regulation and intervention in the postcolonial world. To view these consequences of human rights claims and discourses as the ideological misuse or abuse of human rights would already be to approach the question of understanding human rights with a certain set of assumptions. These assumptions would be based upon an idea that universal human rights claims necessarily challenge entrenched power relations and are an important mechanism of advocacy on behalf of the victims of abuses or those excluded from traditional frameworks of representation. However, prior assumptions, of the purity of universal human rights claims (and of their potential abuse by powerful actors), are increasingly seen to be problematic.

Human rights claims cannot, in themselves, be accurately seen as either enforcing or challenging the existing relations of power. The one thing that can be asserted with confidence is that human rights claims conflate an ethical or moral claim with a legal and political one. The discourse of the 'human' belongs to the sphere of abstract universal ethics, while that of 'rights' belongs to the framework of a concretely constituted legal and political sphere. In conflating the two spheres, human rights claims pose a challenge to rights as they are legally constituted. The content of this challenge, whether it has any consequences, and, if it does have consequences what these consequences are, are matters for concrete analysis. To suggest that any challenge to the framework of legally constituted rights is necessarily an effective one, or necessarily a good or progressive one, would clearly be naive.

In fact, it was the challenge of naivety of universalist claims that was famously articulated by Jeremy Bentham, the utilitarian philosopher, when he denounced the idea of human rights as 'nonsense on stilts'. He had nothing but contempt for the newfangled universal 'rights of man' proclaimed at the end of the eighteenth century.[1] For Bentham, rights meant nothing unless they were enforceable with clear contractual obligations and backed by law. Declarations of the 'rights of man' were no more than rhetorical fancies and collections of pious wishes, which were not worth the paper they were written on. The idea that we were born with universal equal rights simply because we were human made no sense to Bentham. Firstly, we are born into a relationship of dependency rather than equality, and are not considered as moral or legal equals until we reach maturity (children are not born with criminal liability as they are not responsible for their actions). Secondly, it was clear that there could be no universal human equality: the opportunities we have depend fundamentally on the societies we live in and our position within those societies. As Kate Nash implies the 'right to rights' is a product of social, historical, and political contestation.

In recent years human rights have often been problematised if they are understood in top-down or social democratic ways, which are held to ignore the social, historical, and cultural preconditions necessary for the 'right to rights'. As World Bank policy advisor, Oxford professor Paul Collier argues, rights regimes, in some contexts, are not a solution to political conflict but rather a catalyst for it.[2] More radical social theorists, such as Bruno Latour, have also critically engaged with modernist modes of rights understanding. He persuasively argues that Western societies have forgotten the lengthy processes that enabled them to establish liberal rights regimes, which depend on the establishment of a political culture that has to be steadily maintained, renewed, and extended and cannot be exported or imposed.[3]

This shift away from formal universalist understandings of democracy and human rights is increasingly evidenced in the shifting understanding of human rights-based approaches to empowerment. When empowerment was seen as an external provision of legal and political mechanisms for claims, it was subject to failure and not seen to be sustainable. Human rights-based non-governmental organizations now increasingly seek not to empower people to access formal institutional mechanisms but to enable them to empower themselves. This approach places the emphasis on the agency and self-empowerment of local actors themselves, not on the introduction of formal frameworks of rights and provisions, supported by international human rights norms. It is often argued that empowering local actors themselves, evades the moral imperialism of imposing Western human rights norms, but also avoids the moral relativism of merely accepting local traditional practices.[4] It seems possible that we will increasingly see human rights as a pragmatic approach to empowerment that does not necessarily take the universalist and abstract forms associated with either natural rights or with social democratic provisions.[5]

Notes

1. Jeremy Waldron ed., *'Nonsense Upon Stilts': Bentham, Burke and Marx on the Rights of Man* (London: Routledge, 1987).
2. Paul Collier, *Wars, Guns and Votes: Democracy in Dangerous Places* (London: Vintage, 2010).
3. Bruno Latour, *An Inquiry into Modes of Existence: An Anthropology of the Moderns* (Cambridge, MA: Harvard University Press, 2013).
4. Diane Gillespie and Molly Melching, "The Transformative Power of Democracy and Human Rights in Nonformal Education: The Case of Tostan," *Adult Education Quarterly* 60, no. 5 (2010): 477–98. doi:10.1177/0741713610363017.
5. David Chandler "Resilience and the 'Everyday': Beyond the Paradox of 'Liberal Peace,'" *Review of International Studies* 41, no. 1 (2015): 27–48. doi:10.1017/S0260210513000533.

5

Human Rights and the Paradoxes of Liberalism

Costas Douzinas

Human rights are a hybrid of liberal law, morality, and politics. Their ideological power lies in their ambiguity, not in their adherence to liberal values of individual freedom.

Human rights are the last universal ideology after the proclaimed end of ideology and history. They unite the North and the South, the Church and the state, first-world liberals and third-world revolutionaries. Human rights are used as a symbol for liberalism, capitalism, or individualism by some and for development, social justice, or peace by others. In the South, rights are seen as primarily collective rather than individual, social and economic rather than civil, associated with equality rather than liberty.

Does the victory and ubiquity of rights indicate that they transcend conflicts of interests and the clash of ideas? Have rights become a common horizon uniting Cardiff and Kabul, London and Lahore? It is a comforting idea, daily denied in news bulletins. If there is something perpetual about our world, it is not Kant's peace but the increasing wealth gap between North and

South, between rich and poor, and the mushrooming and strictly policed security walls dividing the wealthy from the underclass of immigrants, refugees, and the allegedly undeserving poor.

The protests and uprisings that broke out earlier this decade all over the world demanded social justice and equality not human rights ('We are the 99 percent', 'stop austerity and cuts'). The absence of appeals to human rights gives us the opportunity to revisit their theoretical and political premises. Human rights is a combined term. Legal rights have been the building block of Western law since early modernity modelled on the right to property, the first and still most significant right. As human, rights introduce a type of morality in the way public and now private powers should treat people. The legitimacy of modern law was based on its claim to be ideologically neutral, beyond morality, ideology, and politics. The proliferation of human rights marks the realisation that state law could be bent to the most atrocious policies. Human rights are therefore a hybrid category of liberal law and morality. But as morality is not one and the law is not a simple exercise in reasoning, moral conflict enters the legal archive and legal strictures regiment moral responsibility. As a result a number of paradoxes enter the heart of society by bringing together law and morality. Let me offer five theses developing some of the paradoxes.

Thesis 1   Human rights classify people on a spectrum between the fully human, the lesser human, and the inhuman.

Liberals claim that human rights are given to people on account of their humanity instead of membership of narrower categories such as state, nation, or class. If that were the case, refugees, undocumented immigrants, the Guantánamo Bay prisoners who have no state or law to protect them should be prime beneficiaries of the consolations of humanity. They have very few. 'Bare' humanity offers no protection and whoever claims to represent it lies.[1] Humanity has no fixed or universally acceptable meaning and cannot act as the source of moral or legal rules. Historically, the barbarians for the Greeks and Romans, the heathen for the Christians, the uncivilized for the imperialists, the irrational racial and sexual minorities for the privileged, the illegal immigrants for the citizens, or the economically redundant for the affluent have been divisions of humanity. Human rights help construct who and how one becomes human.

Thesis 2   Power and morality, sovereignty and rights are not fatal enemies as is often argued. Instead a historically specific amalgam of sovereignty and morality forms the structuring order of each epoch and society.

Natural rights, the early modern predecessor of human rights, were a necessary companion of the nation state and nationalism. The French 'Declaration of the Rights of Man'[2] stated that 'all men are born free and equal' but gave its universal rights only to French white, male, and propertied citizens. The post-World War II order combined non-intervention in the domestic affairs of states, that is the strongest possible support of national sovereignty, with the claim of universal human rights. As President Reagan said of the Universal Declaration and its social and economic rights, it is akin to a child's letter to Santa. Finally, the post-1989 new world order has pierced the national sovereignty of 'rogue' states nominally to protect citizens from their evil governments. But the aftermath of the Afghanistan and Iraq invasions shows that the spread of democracy and human rights was a flimsy smokescreen. In the past, the 'civilizing mission' included missionaries and gunboats; today, human rights, missiles, and drones. The combination of the huge structural in-equalities and state repression of neoliberal globalization with a legal ideology promising dignity and equality creates a systemic instability leading the so-called 'new world order' to its demise.

Thesis 3 In advanced Western societies, human rights de-politicises politics.

I do not refer here to traditional civil liberties and the limited protections the underprivileged, the oppressed, and the poor still claim and rarely get. This is the core case of civil liberties. The problem lies elsewhere: human rights have lost their signifi-cance and edge by becoming the vernacular expression of every kind of individual aspiration and desire (every 'I want X' can po-tentially become 'I have a right to X') and a dominant language of public policy. The right wing leads the attack by targeting ille-gal immigrants, prisoners, and supposedly bogus refugees while promoting the rights of property owners, bankers, and crime victims. For the defenders of free market individualism, rights are playthings of the middle class. As Labour and the Tories move to the ideological centre, conflict was declared finished. The emphasis on the rights of property owners and consumers pursues the same agenda. It gives the impression that rich bank-ers and the unemployed, or the privacy of the middle class and the basic dignity of the unemployed belong to the same register.

Antagonism is the reality of politics, and social justice its aim. Rights as individual entitlements cannot tackle inequal-ity nor are they synonymous with justice. Indeed liberal ju-risprudence considers social and economic rights secondary because they are not justiciable, that is, their nature makes them somehow inappropriate for litigation. When individual rights become the site and stake of politics, they join the choice agenda and a manifestation of neoliberalism.

Thesis 4   The distance between having a right and enjoying it is huge.

Take the right to work, or the claim that we are all born equal: both mainstays of international treaties. Having a right to work means nothing for the millions of unemployed. Formal rights are silent as regards the preconditions for their exercise. The right to work does not refer to an existing entitlement but to a political claim. In this sense, the politics of rights is always in potential conflict with their legal status. Human rights statements are prescriptions: people are not free and equal but they ought to become so. Only political struggle not the law can achieve this. Equality is a call for action not a description of a state of affairs. Again take the nominally non-controversial right to life. Its statement does not answer questions about abortion, the death penalty, euthanasia, or whether the necessary prerequisites for survival such as food, shelter, or health care should be protected. In most cases, a human rights claim is the beginning rather than the end of a dispute about its meaning or its standing vis-à-vis conflicting rights.

When God—the author of natural law—died, international law replaced him as the source of the latest higher source of morality. The ideological power of human rights lies precisely in their rhetorical and political ambiguity, the oscillation between ideal and real, between humanity and national citizenship, between law's order and the desire for a better world. When human rights are part of the law, the law includes a principle of self-transcendence, which pushes against the law's settled state.

A legal system with human rights is paradoxically not equal to itself, since human rights can call the whole of law to account. In this sense, rights become not the last ideology but the latest expression of the human urge to resist domination and oppression and the intolerance of public opinion. They are part of a long and honourable tradition, which started with Antigone's defiance of unjust law and surfaces in the struggles of the despised, enslaved, or exploited. In this sense, rights have a double meaning and life. They are (legal) claims to be admitted to the privileges of the law and (political) demands to have the whole of the law improved or changed.

Thesis 5 The end of human rights is to resist public and private domination and oppression. They lose that end when they become the political ideology or idolatry of neoliberal capitalism or the contemporary version of the civilizing mission.

Notes

1. Liisa H. Malkki, "Speechless Emissaries: Refugees, Humanitarianism, and Dehistoricization," *Cultural Anthropology* 11, no. 3 (1996): 377–404. doi:10.1525/can.1996.11.3.02a00050.
2. Thomas Paine, "Declaration of the Rights of Man and of Citizens," in *Rights of Man* (Cambridge: Cambridge University Press, 2012): 116–19. doi:10.1017/CBO9781139177672.003.

6

Rights and Power: Illiberal Constitutions of Latin America

Roberto Gargarella

Recent constitutional reforms in Latin America have attracted lots of attention from the world: many of them (and here, the cases of Ecuador, Venezuela, or Bolivia rank first) emerged after processes that were (at least in principle) open to the public and participatory in their nature; and in some cases resulted in unorthodox and challenging constitutions. However, there was at least one crucial problem affecting most of these experiments, which was the following. Many of these reformist processes concentrated their energies in the section of rights, without taking into account the impact that the organization of power tends to have upon those very rights. Latin American Constitutions thus appeared as constitutions with 'two souls': one that established a powerful, renewed, democratic, and progressive set of rights; and the other that consecrated a hierarchical, traditional organization of powers. The problem with this design is that through the vertical political organisation that it builds, the new constitutions tend to undermine the liberal and social promises that they make through their rights-sections. It has usually been the case that powerful executives who concentrate most of the political power in their own hands do not welcome challenges to their concentrated authority coming from civil society. The fact that many of these challenges come (as it happened in recent Latin American history) from groups that ground their demands in particular constitutional provisions has not modified this tendency, but rather reinvigorated it. As a result, we find numerous cases of executive authorities that have limited legal reforms by introducing new amendments or simply by ignoring the constitution's demands. There is not room here to outline these examples—on which I have written extensively elsewhere[1]—but amongst the most telling have been the vetoing of laws that go against extractivist (the large-scale extraction of natural resources) economic policies with their damaging consequences especially for the self-determination of indigenous groups.

Of course, the introduction of changes in rights can generate a huge impact on the ways in which power is distributed. Typically, for example, the extension of the franchise *implies* an extraordinary change in the organization of power. We may say something similar regarding the right to minimum wage, or the right to a union. However, one should note at least two things. First, many rights have the *potential* to expand people's power (the right to join trade unions, the right to minimum wage), but they remain in practice unforced or subenforced, due to pressures exerted from the (unmodified) structure of government. In other cases, such as the right to vote (the most important and also the most peculiar of all), the absence of corresponding changes in the organization of power reveals the way in which constitutions ensure that the levers of power are still driven by a few. Omitting to change the organization of power, reformers have left the new democratic societies under an elitist form of political direction that was typical of the eighteenth century.

It is interesting to contrast this remarkable omission, typical of recent reforms, with what old legal scholars used to do when engaged in a process of constitutional change. In effect, the engineers of the old liberal-conservative compact (typical of the mid-eighteenth century) showed no doubts about what they had to do, in order to ensure the life of their most cherished rights—especially the right to property. For them, it seemed totally clear that in order to guarantee protections to the right to property, the first thing to do was to get into the 'engine room' of the constitution, namely to change the organisation of constitutional powers. Typically, then, they proposed the restriction of political liberties in order to ensure the enjoyment of broader economic freedoms. This was, for example, the main constitutional lesson offered by Juan Bautista Alberdi (one of the greatest constitutional thinkers of Latin America during the nineteenth century): it was necessary to temporarily tie the hands of the majority, so as to ensure protection for certain basic economic rights. By doing so, these old legal thinkers showed that they were totally aware of the need to introduce changes in the organisation of power in order to achieve the enjoyment of certain rights in practice.

I believe that contemporary legal scholars should learn this important lesson from our predecessors: in order to introduce fundamental changes in the constitution—particularly those related to the introduction of more or better social guarantees, or both—one needs to affect the organisation of power, which is presently putting so many obstacles to the enforcement of the new rights incorporated in our texts. The hope for social justice and expanded liberties for oppressed groups depends less on the recognition of more constitutional rights than on the adoption of radical political reforms to open the doors to their claims and voices.

Note

1. Roberto Gargarella, *Latin American Constitutionalism (1810–2010): The Engine Room of the Constitution* (Oxford: Oxford University Press, 2013).

7

Rights: What Are They Good For?

Nivedita Menon

Let us remind ourselves that the notion of rights as we understand them today arose in a specific time/space configuration. It is from the seventeenth century that in Europe individuals began to be seen as autonomous and separate entities. The notion of rights for individuals emerged in modernity both as a vehicle of emancipation from feudal fetters of guilds and communities, and as a means of privileging an emerging bourgeois class within a discourse of formal egalitarianism and universal citizenship. Thus, rights emerged both as a means of protection against arbitrary use and abuse by the sovereign, *and* as a mode of securing the newly emergent dominant social orders of class and gender.

A revealing instance of the slipperiness of the assumed progressive nature of rights is the right to work. What paves the way for the capitalist system, in Marx's view, is primitive accumulation—the process of violently expropriating from the labourer the means of production and transforming it into capital, carried out in Europe in the fifteenth and sixteenth centuries by individual acts of violence. By the eighteenth century, law itself became 'the instrument of theft of people's land'.[1] This process was accompanied by a disciplinary discourse on work that criminalized and brutally punished the refusal to perform labour. Early colonial policy also used the policy of forced labour, particularly in Africa. The intervening centuries and developments in the global capitalist order have seen a radical reversal of this discourse. From the disciplinary discourse of the obligation to work, resisted by the target population, gradually there emerged the social and economic order in which work is unavailable, and all means of self-employment have been destroyed. The resistance of the propertyless to this order is manifested in struggles for the right to work. In short, capitalism initially had to discipline populations into labour, but could never produce enough employment for the vast numbers that were dispossessed and proletarianised. The phenomenon of unemployment having been created, the conditions of possibility emerged in which the right to work could be articulated. The emergence of this right, as of other rights, thus cannot be seen as a simple moment of historical progress.

In India the colonial intervention decisively transformed indigenous notions of justice and brought them in-line with the requirements of modern legal discourse. Rights in the modern sense were produced by colonial transformation of judicial discourse and administrative institutions. The language of rights did empower many subaltern sections against indigenous elites, but it is evident that its emergence was not unambiguously and universally emancipatory. As the work of many historians shows, the new language of rights had devastating consequences for many. For instance, it was through the language of rights that an alliance between British Victorian morality and the male elite of the matrilineal Nair community started the process of legally ending matriliny—pitting the rights of the wife against those of the sister, the subject of course, being assumed to be the Nair male.

Liberal individualism never became the uncontested core of anti-imperialist struggles for democracy. Whether Gandhi and Ambedkar in India or African socialists like Nyerere and Nkrumah, most nationalist leaders constructed national identities, not through the idea of individual citizenship but through that of communities—caste, religion, ethnic groups. Their language of politics remained non-individualistic. And yet there remained always a tension in postcolonial democracies between the community, defined in different ways, as the bearer of rights and the individual. This tension is evident in the Indian Constitution, for instance, where the Fundamental Rights protect the rights of both the individual and the religious community. Sometimes this leads to contradiction between the two—as when equal rights for women as individuals comes into conflict with religious Personal Laws, all of which discriminate against women. Similarly, the demand for reservations in representative institutions on the basis of group identity—women, castes, or religious communities—fundamentally reshapes the conception of political representation at the core of liberal democracy, that of the individual.

The idea of the individual citizen empowered with rights in the public sphere derived its emancipatory potential precisely from its positioning against feudal absolutism. With the passing of that historical moment in the West, and the mediated and refracted manner in which 'modernity' is encountered in colonial and postcolonial societies, the language of rights has lost much of its relevance. The extension of this language from rights of the individual *against* the state, to the rights of collectivities against one another and against individuals, as well as rights defined in such broad terms as the right to be fully human—these rights to be *guaranteed by* the state—has raised contradictions that have not been adequately confronted.

Take for instance the universal rights/multiculturalism dichotomy. The rights discourse does not permit us to challenge both ends of this dichotomy—the reification of cultural boundaries by the discourse of multiculturalism as well as the unproblematic assertion of universal rights by its opponents.

We know by now that an unqualified defence of the notion of universal human rights is all too often linked, in the current world scenario, to the United States of America as the global champion. In the new unipolar world, the choice is posed as one between universal rights protected by good governance, and an anti-human rights position supported by (Islamic) religious fundamentalists or dictators. What this polarization obscures is the fact of internal opposition to dictatorship, and that external action usually ends up strengthening the dictatorial forces, swamping democratic opposition *within* those countries on a tide of resurgent nationalism.

But at the same time, the alternative cannot be a defence of rights for communities assumed to be internally homogeneous. The framework of multiculturalism poses the problem for liberal democracies as one of the *external* relationship of different communities to other communities, to be mediated by the state, when the problem of gender or caste is *internal* to the very constitution of the community itself.

Thus, French feminists *should* hesitate to support the French government's prohibition on wearing the hijab in schools, for this could feed into processes marginalising and demonising the Muslim community. Moreover, the critical voices *internal* to the community may be delegitimized within the community, not strengthened, by open support for the French government's policy from the mainstream feminist movement. In such a scenario, alliances should be between feminists outside and feminists inside the community, not between some feminists and the state.

Feminist critiques of the universalism of international human rights discourses must, in short, equally strongly attack the particularism of the nation state and of the community. Our space will have to be the terrain of solidarities that are simultaneously anti-imperialist, counter-globalisation, and post-nationalist.

Note

1. Karl Marx, *Capital: Critique of Political Economy*, trans. Ben Fowkes, vol. 1, *The Process of Capitalist Production* (London: Penguin Books, 1990).

8

Sexual Subalterns, Human Rights, and the Limits of the Liberal Imaginary

Ratna Kapur

In the contemporary struggle for justice and equality by sexual subalterns through the edifice of human rights, we are witnessing a polarized response that requires deeper interrogation. At one end, there is an increased criminalization of queer lives, where not just the sex act, but the very identity of homosexuals are criminalised, such as in Nigeria, Uganda, Kenya, Ethiopia, the Democratic Republic of Congo, and Russia. At the opposite end of the spectrum, the struggle for rights claims has challenged the pathologising and criminalising of homosexuality, resulting in legal recognition in countries such as Nepal, Cambodia, South Africa, several European countries, and a number of US states. The ultimate culmination point of this struggle for legitimacy rests in the recognition of same-sex marriages.

In the choice between criminality and legitimacy, legitimacy seems clearly preferable. The struggle for legal recognition would seem an obvious strategy given that it affords access, public standing, and legibility—all of which are essential ingredients for effective democratic participation. In the context of homosexuality, is it better to have legal recognition, including the option to get married as a gay person, as opposed to having an active law that persecutes not only homosexual conduct but the very identity of homosexuals as is happening in Nigeria, Uganda, Kenya, and elsewhere? Can there be any reasonable argument against invoking human rights to challenge legal provisions that call for life imprisonment or the death penalty for being gay? The answer is clearly no. It is better not to be persecuted.

At the same time, the pursuit of human rights as a liberating and emancipatory force needs to be further interrogated through the optics of a critically queer postcolonial lens. Firstly, if gay marriage is permissible in the United States, Canada, or France, it cannot be based on the one-dimensional reasoning that these societies are just better, more civilized, and mature than say Uganda or Nigeria. Such reasoning deflects attention, for example, from the way in which Christian evangelicals from the United States have been implicated in partly producing an anti-gay agenda in these African nations. They have been driving an agenda that is received within a context where conservative sexual and gender norms constituted partly by the legacies of the colonial past continue to resonate in the postcolonial present.

Secondly, a position that continues to associate justice through the pursuit of human rights with the West while African countries and their leaders are cast as retrogressive and barbaric does not implicate the way in which human rights operates against a normative agenda on both sides of this equation. There continues to exist a position across these divides that abhors homosexuality and the homosexual. He or she must be put down or not served because it is against one's religious convictions—exemplified in the recent, though failed, efforts of the Arizona state legislature. Or in France, where the legalization of same-sex marriage witnessed some of the largest protests in Paris since the 1960s, opposing the law, coupled with an upsurge of homophobic violence against the gay community. The Paris protests illustrate that homosexuals continue to be regarded as not fully developed subjects within that cultural and political space, despite legal recognition. Dominant Catholic theological notions partly constitute the liberal subject and the frames of recognisability that determine who is entitled to legal recognition and rights, and who is not.

The broader issue is that decriminalising homosexuality does not in and of itself equate with liberation and incorporation into a space of freedom and happiness. It is a release into a competing normative order that disciplines and tames the way in which one can be in the world. Sexuality and sexual desire continue to be cabined or constrained against governing sexual, gender, and cultural norms.

Thirdly, international LGBT human rights advocacy has not necessarily challenged the framework within which precarious desires and sexual subalterns are addressed and have at times reproduced the binary between those who are progressive and civilized, and those societies that remain in a state of transition until the human rights of LGBT persons are secured. Opposing discrimination in Uganda, Nigeria, and India may take place on terms that accept the idea that homophobia is endemic to Islam or civilisationally immature countries. These interventions also tend to assume something about freedom and what freedom should look like—that is—outness as opposed to the closet.

The analysis compels those involved in sexual rights advocacy to interrogate their faith in human rights as a progressive project, and reflect on how such advocacy may simultaneously trigger coercive norms that operate to exclude other disadvantaged or discriminated groups, while also re-producing cultural and civilisational divides. A similar critique has been made of women's human rights advocacy. Sexual freedom, like women's freedom, comes to be advocated partly through the restriction and exclusion of religious expression or demonising of the cultural other. Injustice is not clarified by linking it to essentialist assumptions about culture and religion. It takes us no further along the road in understanding the features that produce such discriminations and that cannot be limited to conservative sexual morality or culture.

While human rights, which frame the subject and under-standings of freedom strictly within a liberal imaginary, appear to be something that we cannot not want (to paraphrase Gayatri Spivak, writing in a different context),[1] it is important to add that they cannot give us what we want. The conferment of recognition of subjectivity in a global context through human rights can move in the direction of becoming a totalised response and invite regulation of these once radical subjectivities. What is important to recognise is that this move, while different from one that criminalises and outlaws, is also constraining. It is not self-evident that recognition and legitimacy equate to the idea of human rights as a progressive end goal. Instead, human rights operate to uphold a specific normative order, which continue to regulate, discipline, and monitor the sexual 'other'.

Note

1. Gayatri Chakravorty Spivak, *Outside in the Teaching Machine* (New York, Routledge, 1993).

9

Human Rights and Its Inherent Liberal Relativism

Abdullahi An-Na'im

By liberal relativism I mean the set of values and institutions that limit human rights to negative claims on the state to refrain from interfering with the freedom of individuals. This perspective upholds civil and political rights of citizens, pays lip service to notions of inclusive universality of human rights, and relegates economic and social rights and collective demands for development and protection of the environment to the realm of aspirational policy. In this model, judicially enforceable negative civil and political rights are true rights, while affirmative claims on the state for economic and social justice are deemed incidental outcomes of upholding true rights. By imposing its own relativist conception of rights, liberalism accuses other paradigms of relativism in order to proclaim its own relativism as universalism.

In reality liberalism is merely one among many possible competing ideological and cultural relativisms and should not be allowed to gain priority in order to serve the interests of major powers and the whims of manipulative private and public donors. Liberal relativism is a neo-colonial ploy designed to maintain the exploitation of developing countries by developed former colonial powers. This ploy is also sustained by the so-called 'human rights advocacy' by Northern-based international non-governmental organizations like Amnesty International and Human Rights Watch, which hide the working of neo-colonial structural underlying causes of human rights violations by failing to expose those realities.

This view is relativist because it is premised on a particular philosophical view and political experience. It is neo-colonial because it projects that relativist view as universal through imperial hegemony, economic blackmail, and the constant implicit threat of use of military force at the discretion of the same former colonial powers, while 'international' finance and US-backed loan businesses make it impossible for 'developing' countries to realize socio-economic and cultural rights. The liberal scenario is paradoxical because it negates the self-determination of poor countries in the name of protecting their human rights. The point here is not whether a claim deserves recognition as a human right or not, but that the imperialist coercive nature of the process does not enable consideration of the possibility of a non-liberal perspective.

We all know and experience the world as who we are, men and women of racial, linguistic, cultural, religious, or other affiliation or identity. Since every claim of a human right is relative to all our particularities everywhere, the quality of being a universal norm can neither be assumed nor imposed. A liberal conception of any norm as a human right or not is necessarily as relativist as a religious or communitarian conception of that or any other norm. The paradox of universality is that any enforcement of a norm is a negation of its human rights quality, yet the lack of voluntary compliance is what constitutes a violation of the right. To say that enforcement is justified because the norm is a human right is to beg the question, 'who decides?'. The object of universality is to ensure the protection of certain rights regardless of national constitutional, legal, and political level of protection. Yet, coercive enforcement of these international obligations is neither possible in practice nor acceptable in principle.

The international protection of human rights can work only through the internalisation of those rights as indigenous values in the socialisation of children and interpersonal and communal relations. External protection may appear necessary because both the violation and implementation of human rights always happen within the territorial jurisdiction of one state or another. Yet the intervention itself is a violation of sovereignty. In any case, external actors cannot be present everywhere and long enough to ensure comprehensive, consistent, and sustainable protection of human rights. External actors cannot have the legitimacy, cultural competence, and local access to prevent or remedy violations.

The inadequacy of hegemonic liberal relativism is also clear in that the monitoring and evaluation mechanisms deployed by liberal actors are designed for the negative task of collecting narrow information about violation of a limited number of rights, usually of political elites who are competing over political power in the name of protecting the rights of the poor. Priorities of monitoring violations are determined by what official and private donors are willing to fund, and there is no evaluation of the effectiveness of what is done. The fact that violations of rights are accurately reported does not mean that they will end or be redressed, and there is no follow-up to ensure any specific outcome.

The liberal approach can only work in a piecemeal and reactive manner, responding to human rights violations after they occur, rather than pre-empting them or preventing their occurrence. It also tends to focus on specific cases or limited issues, without attempting to address structural causes of human rights violations or creating institutional mechanisms for sustainable respect for and protection of rights. The whole system of international law and relations and private donors who support the present human rights regime is necessarily opposed to addressing the underlying causes of violations because to do so would threaten the existence of the major actors in both official and private domains.

This critique does not deny the role of present inter-governmental and non-governmental human rights regimes, but only seeks to expose its inherent relativity. Let us acknowledge that all we can have are competing relativisms so that we can begin to debate relative benefits to differently positioned populations. The essential doctrine of human rights can only be realized by entrusting the effort to realize them to the human agency of the subjects of those rights, and shifting action to the essentially political nature of the struggle.[1] National and international legal strategies can only follow political action, never lead or replace it.

Note

1. Joel Beinin and Hossam el-Hamalawy, "Egyptian Textile Workers Confront the New Economic Order," *Middle East Report,* March 25, 2007.

10

Who Is the Human in Human Rights?

Anne Phillips

Who is the human in human rights? In principle, of course, this is anyone and everyone—this is the whole point of claiming rights as a human rather than as a citizen of a particular country—and the rights of this human must apply equally, without hierarchy or discrimination. The language signals the inclusive equality of all human beings, and yet in practice the scope of human rights has been far more limited. Some of the failure reflects a resistance to recognising all humans as genuinely equal. Some reflects a continuing tendency to pattern images of the human on particular subgroups, to see men, for example, as generic humans, and to find it much more difficult to see women in this way. The greatest difficulty, however, is that the language of the human offers us equality at the price of abstracting from all our differences. It tells us that it shouldn't matter whether we are male or female, Hutu or Tutsi, Muslim, Christian, or Jew, for we are all of us human beings. This is a powerful ethical ideal, and the world would surely be a better place than it currently is if people really acted on it. Yet the injunction to set our differences aside falls a long way short of what is ultimately needed to achieve the kind of equality promised in the language of human rights. In the conventional liberal version, the human in human rights *has* to be an abstraction in order to deliver equality: we have to abstract mentally from everything we otherwise know in order to recognise others as our equals. The problem with this is that it too often remains an empty ethical imperative, incapable of dealing with the institutionalised power relations that currently mark us as unequal. What we need, rather, is to be able to hold together—often in tension— the requirements of both equality *and* difference.

When the French revolutionaries declared the 'Rights of Man and the Citizen', they were at least honest enough to specify their own restrictions. They did not commit themselves to the view that all humans are born free and equal (it was men and citizens), and though in the fervour of the revolutionary years, they subsequently voted to extend the rights to Protestants as well as Catholics, Jews as well as Christians, they continued to resist the suggestion that French women could be as fully citizens as French men. With the later declarations, made explicitly in the name of the human, one might anticipate an end to all restriction, but as feminist critics of the human rights industry have repeatedly argued, even here there have been question marks over who qualifies. One element in this is scope. Human rights clearly include the right not to be tortured; but can we seriously claim it as a *human* right to be able to vote when convicted of a criminal offence, to sleep with someone of the opposite sex, or to live amicably with one's partner without facing daily violence? Those contesting the extensions point out—with some justification—that human rights may lose their weight and significance if stretched to cover everything we consider desirable; they then arbitrarily apply this dictum to exclude what they regard as too trivial or private to count. Much of the feminist engagement with the politics of human rights has then centred on the failure to recognise private violations of rights as of the same status as public ones; and many of the advances of recent years have occurred around the growing acceptance that rape, for example, is a violation of human rights when perpetrated by private individuals as well as by agents of the state, or genital cutting a violation of human rights even though performed in the privacy of the home.

The other element is a continuing resistance to recognising women as generic humans. Violations of the rights of women or children are taken far more seriously today, but note how often they are described precisely as that: as violations of *women's* rights, or *children's* rights, as if these fall into a different category from violations of the rights of the human. When women and men alike face torture or arbitrary imprisonment, we talk of violations of their human rights, and may well conjure up images of men as the typical victims. When women are the only victims of a particular violation, we tend, rather, to talk of violations of women's rights. Even today, that is, after many years of campaigning under the slogan 'women's rights are human rights too', it is easier for men than for women to serve as the generic human.

One might plausibly think that if this is the problem, the solution lies in more rigorous abstraction, and that we should now set out about stripping away all remaining remnants of maleness, or whiteness, or whatever other dominant characteristic has illegitimately crept into the supposedly generic human. The problem is that this may also deprive us of the resources we need to address inequalities, for the separation between abstract human core and supposedly inessential difference commonly works to shore up relations of power. Iris Marion Young argued in *Justice and the Politics of Difference*[1] that when we call on people to bracket out their particularities, to think beyond their markers of difference and merely local grievances and concerns, we usually end up affirming the dominance of the already dominant. It is those on the margins who are most characterised by and preoccupied with difference, and the power hierarchies that trouble their lives do not disappear when they invoke the notion of the human. Liberal conceptions of human rights sometimes seem trapped between overly substantive notions of the human that serve to exclude (or occlude) major subsets of humanity, and overly abstract notions that wish away the significance of difference. The challenge is to develop a human rights politics that delivers on the inclusive equality of all human beings without, in the process, obliterating the differences or rendering us all the same.[2]

Notes

1. Iris Marion Young, *Justice and the Politics of Difference* (Princeton, NJ: Princeton University Press, 1990).
2. For a fuller development of this argument, see Anne Phillips, *The Politics of the Human* (Cambridge: Cambridge University Press, 2015).

11

The European Court of Human Rights:
Would Marx Have Endorsed It?

Başak Çalı

It's not hard to find a critic of the European Court of Human Rights these days. I have no intention, in this chapter, of joining this increasingly voluble choir of nationalists, fearmongers, and far-right or authoritarian regimes. What I want to do is to approach the European Court of Human Rights in the context of the relationship between human rights and liberalism, in particular market liberalism, and ask whether Marx would have endorsed the European Court of Human Rights as an intrinsic human good for Europeans.

Could the European Court of Human Rights have convinced Marx that it has succeeded in lifting the veil on abstract rights masking substantive injustices as per his critique of rights in *Capital*? To what extent has it fought against civil rights becoming a banner for liberal egoism and individualism as per 'On the Jewish Question'?

There is nothing new in saying that the European Convention on Human Rights was created to fight fascist and authoritarian political regimes and to lock European states into forms of democratic and politically liberal forms of government. Indeed, the phrase 'necessary in a democratic society' appears[1] in the text of the Convention multiple times when the Convention seeks to restrict rights of expression, association, assembly, privacy, and religion. This suggests that the core purpose of the European Court of Human Rights is to fight the real-time ills of a lack of political liberalism in European societies. The market and the failures of economic liberalism, however, are not part of the purposive development of the Court. Further than this, as seen in the Strasbourg Court's developing doctrine of deference to democratic parliaments (*S.A.S v. France*), the primacy of democratic decision making in the court's case law suggests that as long as the market economy is endorsed by some form of democratic citizen participation (*Hatton v. UK*), the European Court of Human Rights is happy to let markets be markets.

The only heuristic channel though which the European Court of Human Rights addresses market liberalism is when the consequences of market liberalism pose a danger to its effective rights interpretation doctrine. With a commitment to effective, not abstract, rights, the European Court of Human Rights crosses paths with Marx's critique of liberal rights in *Capital.* In the now landmark *Airey v. Ireland* judgment of 1979, the European Court of Human Rights stood up against the abstractness of Irish domestic law when rejecting the Irish government's argument that a woman who cannot afford a lawyer in divorce proceedings would still get a fair trial. In paragraph twenty-four of the judgment the court declared that 'the Convention is intended to guarantee not rights that are theoretical or illusory but rights that are practical and effective.' In doing so it opened the door for the creation of a social, context-sensitive and concrete theory of human rights as opposed to an abstract liberal theory of rights devoid of any context. Thousands of applicants after

Airey have told the Court that they did not *really* enjoy rights while homosexuality was criminalised (*Dudgeon v. UK*), when rape was not investigated (*MC v. Bulgaria*), or when their families (*Vallianatos and Others v. Greece*) or trade unions (*Demir and Baykara v. Turkey*) were not recognised.

This, however, is indeed a mere crossing of paths. While a Marxist critique of abstract rights turns largely on the abstract forms masking substantive injustices perpetrated by the political economy of liberal capitalism, the European Court of Human Rights criticises abstract rights for their failure to deliver real consequences for an applicant. That applicant, however, can range from a company or a group of individuals who cannot access the real value of their property, to a worker.

The effectiveness of rights in European Court of Human Rights case law has since given birth to other progressive doctrines, namely, the living instrument doctrine (*Bayatyan v. Armenia*), autonomous concepts doctrine (*Alexeyev v. Russia*), and the positive obligations doctrine (*Dubetska and Others v. Ukraine*). All of these doctrines, too, offer opportunities for individuals to challenge constantly changing domestic economic policies and demand more from the state to assist them in their individual or collective self-development. These doctrines, however, also do not tie-in to a thicker view about freeing rights from being mirrors of liberal capitalist economic relations.

In this respect the relationship between effective rights and anti-market liberalist agendas is rather hit-and-miss. The *Palomo Sanchez v. Spain* decision illustrates this well. Here, the Court was faced with workers using satirical cartoons of managers to highlight the difficulties they had unionising and to show how domestic Spanish Courts were defending the rights of these managers not to be humiliated. The European Court of Human Rights concluded that the Spanish Courts did not act unreasonably when they weighed the right of employers not to be defamed by employees at work as more valuable than the right to free expression of the employee at the workplace—ultimately deciding that the dismissal of the worker by the employer was a proportionate response. Whilst the case helped to make the rights of managers real and effective, workers' right to expression and work security remained abstract. The European Court of Human Rights did not ask deeper questions about why deference to labour laws structured for an economically liberal system did not pose a challenge to its effective rights doctrine.

How one wants to portray the European Court of Human Rights of course depends on which palette of cases is picked to paint the portrait. What is consistent, though, is that the European Court of Human Rights has given more thought to the necessary conditions for broad political liberal ideals of positive and negative liberties to flourish in democratic settings. The heuristic device of 'effective rights' has worked well for this purpose. When it comes to economic liberalism, however, the European Court of Human Rights is an 'on and off' interlocutor about how law and rights as forms obscure underlying substantive social and economic relations. We may expect it to continue both to demystify and contribute to the 'mystification' of rights[2] on a case-by-case basis.

Notes

1. Christoph Grabenwarter, *European Convention on Human Rights* (Nomos Verlagsgesellschaft mbH & Co. KG, 2014).
2. Karl Marx, *Capital:* Critique of Political Economy, trans. Samuel Moore and Edward Aveling, ed. Frederick Engels, vol. 1, *The Process of Capitalist Production* (New York: International Publishers, 1967), 729–30.

12

Intervention: Imperialism or Human Rights?

Ray Kiely

The issue of intervention, and more specifically of altruistic, liberal intervention has regained its prominence in the post-Cold War era. Interventions—their forms and their justifications—have varied since the early 1990s, but they have usually involved some recourse to the argument that the human rights of individuals are more important than the sovereignty of states. Critics reject intervention irrespective of circumstances, on the grounds that state sovereignty is paramount, cosmopolitanism is instrumentalised by powerful actors in order to impose their will on weaker ones, and that the morality of intervention is undermined by double standards.

Many liberal interventionists contend that such arguments might have applied in the Cold War, but they are far less applicable now. In the past, Western interventions were often carried out to protect authoritarian regimes on the grounds that this was unavoidable in the context of Cold War power politics, but now intervention is said to be less self-interested and targeted at undemocratic regimes with poor human rights records.

Sometimes the argument is made that these interventions remain self-interested and ethical justifications are simply ideological covers for Western interests. However, too often what is not made clear is what these interests are: for instance, the claim that the war in Iraq was really a war for oil is hardly convincing as the United States easily meets its oil requirements irrespective of Iraqi oil, and in any case it is less dependent on Middle East oil than other nations. The argument that interventions are hypocritical because they involve double standards might be true but for interventionists it is beside the point, as it is impossible to intervene in all places at all times. Moreover, the exercise of double standards is a lesser evil than simply allowing dictatorial regimes to continue. In effect cases against intervention made by so-called anti-imperialists all too easily become apologies for dictatorships.

There is plenty of evidence to support this last accusation. The trajectory of the Stop the War Coalition, formed to oppose intervention in Afghanistan and then Iraq is but one example, as its statement on the Ukraine crisis and implicit support for Russia (as my enemy's [US imperialism] enemy is my friend [Russia]) showed. On the other hand the anti-imperialist argument concerning selectivity and double standards cannot be as easily dismissed as the liberal interventionists make out. It is one thing to say that each individual intervention must by its nature be selective, but it is quite another when the United States or Britain actively court allies to the cause of ethical intervention. The coalition of the willing in Iraq in 2003 contained a number of states that had poor human rights records, and too often the United States and its allies have made alliances with states or political movements only to then deem these same allies as evil when circumstances change. This cannot simply be dismissed on the grounds that 'that was then and this is now'. Historical amnesia runs the danger of producing an ever recurring cycle of violence in which yesterday's contingent friends are today's necessary enemies, and today's contingent friends may end up being tomorrow's necessary enemies. Serious questions therefore have to be asked about the West's perception of itself as being the purveyors of freedom and justice, a fact reinforced by a far from noble history of colonialism and bloody intervention.

This latter point brings us to some of the most difficult issues for liberal interventionists. First, as David Runciman's brilliant deconstruction of Tony Blair demonstrates,[1] there is the assumption that good intentions alone are sufficient to justify supposedly unintended actions and outcomes, such as the curiously named 'collateral damage'. These outcomes are then supposedly excused by good intentions, as if the problem—say, civil war in Iraq, or the rise of ISIS—lies with reality, and not the judgement of the liberal interventionist. This distinction between intention and outcome is central to certain strands of liberal political thought, and neoliberalism in particular,[2] but it ignores the question of foresight—in this case the existence of political forces that do not embrace liberal democracy. To recognise the reality of undemocratic outcomes is not to apologise for it, but clearly the moralisation of politics carries with it all kinds of dangers when reality is all but ignored.

Second, liberal interventionists are very naive about the conflict-ridden realities of capitalist (and non-capitalist) development, both in the past and the present. Interventionists should be realistic about the outcomes of interventions, all too often assuming that a foreign military intervention will rapidly be followed by a period of peaceful development. This assumption betrays a key characteristic of neoliberal thought, namely a methodological individualism, which in this specific case reduces the problem of a rogue or failed state to the existence of a single evil individual or political movement. Finally, the overlap between liberal interventionism and neoliberalism can be seen in terms of the further assumption that intervention will be followed by the rise of a politics that naively embraces actually existing globalisation as if this was simply a policy choice without constraint. Liberal interventionists thus often support forms of exclusion, exploitation, and marginalisation that are the product of structured hierarchies and inequalities rather than the deliberate action of an identified individual, but these hierarchies are no less coercive for that.

Where then does this leave the debate? Are we caught between support for liberal intervention, which often has disastrous, unintended, but often foreseeable consequences, on the one hand, and an anti-interventionism where we simply ignore the repression faced by many people, on the other? In some respects that depends on what we actually mean by intervention, for much of the debate has focused almost exclusively on *military* intervention. Much of the debate is polarised around the West, either as the saviour of oppressed peoples from rogue dictators (liberal interventionism), or as the oppressor responsible for all the ills of the developing world (anti-imperialism). This displaces agency in those countries in the developing world, reducing it to being the passive recipient of an omnipotent West. This is not a useful starting point for debate, and instead we need to place people in the developing world at the centre of the analysis. Only then can agents in the West start to rethink the question of solidarity, and thus reconstruct a far more modest and humble understanding of what intervention might bring about and above all what intervention might be.

Notes

1. David Runciman, "The Politics of Good Intentions," *London Review of Books* 25, no. 9 (2003): 3–10.

2. Eugene Miller, *Hayek's The Constitution of Liberty: An Account of Its Argument* (London: The Institute of Economic Affairs, 2010).

13

The Role of 'Best Examples' in Human Rights

Monika Krause

Human rights discourse is shaped by best examples—privileged reference points that make some rights and some violations of human rights stand out among others.

Neither held together by a coherent ideology, liberal or otherwise, nor entirely fluid, our knowledge and practice of human rights is structured among other things by best examples, taken for granted reference points that implicitly shape what is perceived to be a human right, a human rights violation, or human rights work. The right to property and the right to free speech have been among the most influential of such best examples among rights; the prisoner of conscience has been emblematic among victims of human rights violations.

'Legal rights have been the building block of Western law since early modernity modelled on the right to property, the first and still most significant right,' Costas Douzinas has argued in this book. With this he points at an important pattern in the world: while national constitutions and international declarations present rights in the form of long and growing lists, not all rights are born equal. Some rights carry more weight than others and those rights, often linked to the image of a specific kind of violation, shape how human rights are imagined more broadly.

We should not rush to try to aggregate privileged reference points into an ideology that is supposed to provide hidden unity to disparate practices. Categories like Western or modern might suggest more coherence than the evidence allows if we start our investigation of human rights discourse from the bottom-up. Psychologists, starting from the microprocess of cognition, call privileged reference points for a category of objects prototypes or best examples. These are clearly affected by social, cultural, and historical context.[1] Professional communities have their own best examples. Biologists routinely focus attention on specific animals such as the fruit fly, or the mouse, which serve as stand-ins for a broader category of organisms. They call these research objects 'model systems'.[2] The literary canon plays a similar role: it focuses attention on some works rather than others, which then shape how whole genres, such as poems, or novels, are read and imagined.[3]

Like in other fields, the salience of best examples of human rights is sustained by specific professional communities and with that by specific practices; these practices are diverse and they are changing over shorter time frames than the term liberalism would have us believe. Freedom of speech and freedom of religion were perhaps *the* best examples of human rights in the 1970s and 1980s, and prisoners of conscience the most exemplary victims of a human rights violation. We might call this 'liberal' but by doing so we would draw a too easy line from this phase of the Cold War all the way back towards the classics of liberal political philosophy.

To the extent that human rights discourse existed before the Cold War—Samuel Moyn has most forcefully argued it was much less prominent then, and very different[4]—free speech was not at its core in the same way, and free speech is no longer that central today. The focus on free speech was favoured by a specific geopolitical constellation; it was also buttressed by an infrastructure of organizational practices, built by Amnesty International, the OSCE, Helsinki Watch, and PEN International. Amnesty's focus on individual prisoners of conscience was not just an ideological choice, it was tightly linked to its organisational innovation of linking members to each other through the adoption of particular victims.

Not all prototypes for human rights are liberal or individualistic. Business and human rights, for example, has become an important area of human rights practice—a new and distinct genre, so to say. The typical cases in this field—the explosion at the chemical factory in Bhopal, India, prominently among them—are ones where victims are groups of workers and communities who depend on specific ecosystems.

Thinking about prototypes highlights questions about how concrete situations are assimilated to the categories that are read in light of different best examples. There is an internal inequality among cases in terms of how well they fit their prototype and a risk of reducing what is specific about each case. But as other assumptions change, new realities can fit old prototypes.[5]

LGBT rights were once thought to be a cause of special interests quite separate from the mainstream of human rights work but are now quite a central part of it. Because sexual orientation is increasingly accepted as part of who people are rather than a choice that can be legislated against, victims of anti-LGBT legislation have newly become assimilated into the category 'prisoners of conscience'. In some ways victims of legislation targeting people for their sexual practices play a role similar to that of emblematic victims of past periods: LGBT victims are used to construct broader lessons about the way everyone becomes vulnerable when there are no protections for those who are different.

Prototypes in human rights work tend to bring a right, a victim, and a perpetrator together in a powerful image. Perhaps because the image that comes to mind lacks a perpetrator, the starving, the sick, and the unemployed as such have never quite become emblematic of human rights violations.

Best examples also sometimes add a specific response to the image of right, victim, and perpetrator. The historian Paige Arthur has shown this for example for the case of 'transitional justice'.[6] She argues that transitional justice came to prominence in the 1980s and 1990s as a new field in the repertoire of international human rights practice. As an approach, it linked the atrocities associated with dictatorships, the promise of a democratic future with an emphasis on prosecution—as opposed to say redistribution—as a response. This linkage was all the more remarkable because it pushed human rights activists into a role they were initially not used to—working with states instead of against them. Though Arthur stresses that this new area of work was transnational and comparative in its inception, we can ask how it was influenced by some cases more than others, such as Argentina and South Africa.

Best examples don't explain all the selectivity of human rights, but it is worth remembering that ideology is not the only other alternative hypothesis available. Mundane logistical constraints as well as inequality of power and resources also play an important role in the process by which indeterminate and contradictory values are translated into practice.

Notes

1. Eviatar Zerubavel, *Social Mindscapes: An Invitation to Cognitive Sociology* (Cambridge, MA: Harvard University Press, 1999).

2. Angela N. H. Creager, Elizabeth Lunbeck and M. Norton Wise, *Science without Laws: Model Systems, Cases, Exemplary Narratives* (Chapel Hill, NC: Duke University Press, 2007), 1–20.

3. Mary Poovey, "The Model System of Contemporary Literary Criticism," *Critical Inquiry* 27, no. 3 (2001), 408–38.

4. Samuel Moyn, *The Last Utopia: Human Rights in History* (Cambridge, MA: Harvard University Press, 2010).

5. Clifford Bob, *The International Struggle for New Human Rights* (Philadelphia: University of Pennsylvania Press, 2008).

6. Paige Arthur, "How 'Transitions' Reshaped Human Rights: A Conceptual History of Transitional Justice," *Human Rights Quarterly* 31, no. 2 (2009), 321–67.

II

Liberalism and Media

We hear a good deal these days about the 'liberal media', much of it critical. In the United States it has long been a reflex action of the conservative Right to condemn loudly much of broadcasting and the press as a nest of 'pinkos'. In Britain a similar line is taken by the Murdoch press, and by—the *Mail*, the *Express*, and the *Telegraph*—against the BBC and the *Guardian*. Meanwhile, critics such as Edward Herman, Noam Chomsky, John Pilger, and Media Lens argue that the media are nothing like as liberal as their right-wing critics claim. And just to make things more complicated, those who want to deregulate public service broadcasting, particularly in the United Kingdom, often talk in terms of liberalising the broadcasting system—by which they mean replacing regulations designed to ensure the existence of a media sphere whose function is to protect and enhance citizens' communicative rights with regulations designed to further the economic interests of media corporations whose sole concern is the extraction of revenue from advertisers and consumers.

It's clear here, then, that the word 'liberalism' is being used in different ways by different people in relation to media systems. To put it at its simplest, it is being marshalled by some to denote a particular form of ideology, which they either support or dislike, whilst others are employing it in a primarily economic sense as part of an argument for changing the way in which broadcasting operates and is organised in Britain and in other western European societies. In such a situation, a large number of questions suggest themselves as possible topics for debate. For example, what is generally meant by 'liberal values' in media terms? Are such values in fact the values proper to journalism, if it is understood as a Fourth Estate? If so, how might they be best protected, encouraged, and enhanced? Is the market the most effective guarantor of the freedom of the press, or can and do market forces act as agents of censorship in certain important respects? And, specifically in the case of much (but not all) of the national press in the United Kingdom, how is it that papers so firmly wedded to economic liberalism, in both its classical and 'neo' forms, are so profoundly illiberal in social terms?

14

The Modalities of Media Liberalism

Julian Petley

Liberalism is a notoriously difficult term to define, meaning different things in different countries and in different eras. As Duncan Bell argues:

> Across and within scholarly discourses, it is construed in manifold and contradictory ways: as an embattled vanguard project and constitutive of modernity itself, a fine-grained normative political philosophy and a hegemonic mode of governmentality, the justificatory ideology of unrestrained capitalism and the richest ideological resource for its limitation. Self-declared liberals have supported extensive welfare states and their abolition; the imperial civilising mission and its passionate denunciation; the necessity of social justice and its outright rejection; the perpetuation of the sovereign state and its transcendence; massive global redistribution of wealth and the radical inequalities of

the existing order. ... Liberalism has become the meta-category of Western political discourse.[1]

More specifically, in an economic and classical sense, liberalism is associated with Adam Smith, Thomas Malthus, and David Ricardo who, in the late eighteenth and early nineteenth centuries, advocated the application of market principles to economic life; its modern form, neoliberalism, calls for their application to all forms of public provision as well. Such policies are generally the province of parties of the Right, although in certain countries they have also been embraced by centre-left parties, most notably in Britain but also in Australia, New Zealand, and Germany, for example.

However, the word liberal has also come to acquire quite different connotations outside the economic sphere, where it is frequently used in ways that make it virtually synonymous with 'social democratic' or even 'progressive'. As Colin Crouch explains in *The Strange Non-Death of Neoliberalism*: 'By the end of the nineteenth century, bourgeois property ownership and the associated liberal right to own factories and other bases of economic activity, including that to employ labour, had themselves become sources of domination and power.'[2] Those subject to this process had begun to seek protection from it, just as the bourgeoisie had once sought to be free from the state, and they looked to that state, which was beginning to become more democratic, as a source of countervailing power. Thus the liberal tradition split in two, with the birth of social liberalism, which in the United Kingdom was associated with T. H. Green, L. T. Hobhouse, and John Hobson and was concerned with efforts to ameliorate the worst consequences of unfettered capitalism, especially for the poor, and which increasingly looked to traditional liberalism's old enemy, the state, for help in this respect. They argued that the state should intervene in public life so that every individual could exercise that right to liberty so dear to liberals and play their full part in society. In the mid-twentieth century such ideas would find their fullest expression in the notion of the welfare state, but would come to be reviled by the Right in the United States, and increasingly by sections of Conservative opinion in the United Kingdom, as little short of crypto-communism.

In media terms, complaints from Conservatives in the United States about liberal media bias are so commonplace that Joe Conason asked in his book *Big Lies*: 'Is there a literate adult living in this country who hasn't heard or read that dull, deceptive phrase literally hundreds or even thousands of times?'[3] And this was before the birth of the Tea Party. That this is vociferously supported by the distinctly illiberal Fox News is, of course, conveniently overlooked by Conservatives, as is the fact that one of the main reasons why the phrase has such currency is that it is endlessly repeated in the press and on television by those self-same Conservatives who habitually complain that their voices are routinely shut out of the media.

In the United Kingdom, the situation is rather different, since so much of the national press is both highly Conservative and, in a social sense, profoundly *illiberal*. So here the anti-liberal battle is waged ceaselessly against only certain specific media outlets, namely those perceived by the Right to be overly liberal—that is the *Guardian*, the BBC and, to a lesser extent these days, Channel 4—with the right-wing press either leading the charge or amplifying attacks made by right-wing politicians. However, if journalism is a modern-day expression of the Enlightenment project (which, after all, gave birth to liberalism in the first place), and if the core purpose of that project is rational enquiry in order to explain the society, and indeed the world in which we live, then journalism must surely privilege reason, proof, argument, accountability, accuracy, truthfulness, and scepticism—particularly towards received opinions and common-sense explanations of social reality. These are in fact core liberal values in a social sense, and represent the underpinnings of what journalists fondly refer to as the Fourth Estate, but they are more a matter of methodology than of ideology, which is why it's perfectly possible to be a Conservative journalist or a socialist journalist and to embrace these values wholeheartedly (for example, Peter Oborne and Paul Foot respectively).

Entirely unsurprisingly, given its political and ideological complexion, the majority of the national press in the United Kingdom defends its freedom not in terms of social but classical liberalism, as has been loudly demonstrated by its daily jeremiads against state censorship ever since the Leveson Inquiry was set up. In this view of things the function of the media, in this case the press, is to provide the information, evidence, and opinion that people need in order to be able to function as citizens, and also to ensure that government does not abuse its power. Thus freedom from government, along with private ownership, are absolutely vital, and the press must be able to compete freely in an open market. The success or failure of newspapers should depend solely on whether or not they can attract sufficient audiences in order to produce a profit. Freedom to publish in the free market will ensure that the press reflects a wide range of opinions and interests in society. If certain viewpoints predominate in the press then this is because they represent popular opinion, and if others are missing this is down to the fact that they lack sufficient following to sustain them in the marketplace.

However, critics of this classical liberal view of press freedom argue that it reduces the notion to little more than a property right, that is, the right to own a newspaper and to do with it whatever one pleases. Further, they claim that by concentrating solely on the state as the enemy of press freedom, classical liberalism ignores the ways in which market forces act as serious constraints on the press, and indeed as a form of censorship. Thus there are very considerable economic barriers to entry to the press marketplace, in which certain players are far more powerful than others. Reliance on advertising funding favours certain kinds of readerships and certain kinds of journalism and discriminates against others. In spite of the much vaunted claims of consumer sovereignty in the newspaper market, diversity of content, reader choice, and public accountability have all been reduced by the dominance of that market by oligopolies.

However, it is abundantly clear that, for neoliberals, the press provides the model of how broadcasting too should be organised in the future: the BBC licence fee should be replaced by subscription, media ownership restrictions abolished, and regulations strictly limited to facilitating the profitable making and selling of programmes (or rather products) in national and international markets. Inevitably such sentiments have found their loudest expression in the pages of newspapers whose owners would stand to gain enormously by the effective abolition of public service broadcasting, and few have noted that such a seismic change in the way in which broadcasting is organised in this country could not be undertaken without massive intervention by the state—intervention of precisely the kind that classical liberals and neoliberals profess to loathe and despise. But as Jonathan Hardy points out in *Critical Political Economy of the Media*:

> The issue is not state vs. market—but what kinds of state policy interventions are made and on whose behalf. ... Marketisation, the opening up of space for private enterprise, is not the result of autonomous, 'natural' free markets or the logical outcome of converging technologies, but is constructed by the decisions (or non-decisions) of public authorities.[4]

What lies behind the endlessly repeated demands for the 'deregulation' of broadcasting is in fact *re-regulation*, namely the replacement of regulations designed to ensure the existence of a media sphere whose function is to protect and enhance citizens' communicative rights by regulations designed to further the economic interests of media corporations whose sole concern is the extraction of revenue from advertisers and consumers.[5]

A number of questions thus pose themselves, some of which are addressed by the chapters in this section. For example, what are the values proper to journalism, and how might these best be protected, encouraged, and enhanced? Are these liberal values in a social sense, or, if not, what are they? Is the market the most effective guarantor of the freedom of the press so highly prized by liberals, or do market forces act as agents of censorship in certain important respects? And, specifically in the case of much (but not all) of the national press in the United Kingdom, how is it that papers so firmly wedded to economic liberalism, in both its classical and 'neo' forms, are so profoundly illiberal in social terms?

Notes

1. Duncan Bell, "What is Liberalism?," *Political Theory* 42, no. 6 (2014): 683. doi:10.1177/0090591714535103.
2. Colin Crouch, *The Strange Non-Death of Neoliberalism* (Cambridge: Polity, 2013), 4.
3. Joe Conason, *Big Lies: The Right-Wing Propaganda Machine and How It Distorts the Truth* (New York: Thomas Dunne Books, 2003), 29.
4. Jonathan Hardy, *Critical Political Economy of the Media: An Introduction* (London: Routledge, 2014), 179.
5. Ibid.

15

Liberalism and the Media

Robert W. McChesney

Many people on the Left of my generation—I came of age in the late 1960s and early 1970s—had a complex relationship with liberalism. Liberals were the targets of Phil Ochs's 'Love Me, I'm a Liberal' song: cowards who talk a good game but never back it up when it conflicts with power, especially capital. Liberals were 'limousine liberals', upper-middle-class people unwilling to risk anything substantial for their values. They were dilettantes.

This was an incomplete representation and rather misleading. Many of the great champions of labour, civil rights, and peace were all diehard liberals, in the New Deal/social democratic sense of the term. The line between them and radicals was often very fuzzy. And among the champions of labour, civil rights, and peace there were no self-described Conservatives to be found. The Conservative tradition was and is entirely unsympathetic to the plight of the dispossessed—except as a rhetorical necessity determined by the audience and the times, or as rank opportunism, as in the case of privatizing schools. So whatever liberalism's flaws, it was a damned sight better than the mainstream alternative.

I never had any particular animus toward liberals. My attitude toward liberalism was strongly influenced by the work of C. B. Macpherson.[1] Macpherson was centrally concerned with the relationship of capitalism to democracy, or inegalitarian economics to egalitarian politics. He termed this the problem of liberal democracy. He was also concerned with what he regarded as the deterioration of the best of the liberal tradition under capitalist auspices. Perhaps most importantly, Macpherson's work paved the way for understanding why contemporary US-style democracy is necessarily weak, and depoliticisation is necessarily rampant. He argued that a corporate capitalist democracy can be stable only if decisions are made by the few with only superficial mass participation, and if liberal values wilt on the vine. In this sense, depoliticisation, demoralisation, and cynicism are rational responses by the bulk of the citizenry to their actual amount of power.

Macpherson pointed out the paternalism and elitism in elements of liberalism, the notion that enlightened intellectuals are the proper rulers of the world. No one has done a better job of showing the strain of contempt for genuine democracy that exists within aspects of liberalism, and how such liberals truly fear popular rule. But what Macpherson also highlighted was the progressive and humanistic impulse of liberalism. I found this notion of liberalism extremely attractive and worth fighting for. He argued that modern capitalism was forcing liberalism to a moment of truth, where it had to decide which of its values it wished to preserve and promote, those of a flawed corporate system or those promoting its democratic ideals. I could not agree more.

Macpherson wrote his main works several decades ago, but the argument is far more true today than it was then. The best liberal values—for example, individual freedoms, the rule of law—are under sharp attack and appear increasingly incapable of surviving the marriage to capitalism.

This tension arguably is more true with regard to the media than to anything else. My own work has been all about driving a truck through the crack in the wall that Macpherson opened. The best of liberal theory is all about having an independent press system that monitors those in power and provides the necessary information to those without property so that they can effectively engage in the exercise of self-government. All the cherished individual freedoms grow out of the strength of democratic rule, and hence the press system. Here, to condense a career's work of research by myself and many others, the really existing capitalist model for media has been an abject failure. Here a commitment to liberal values requires a commitment to the establishment of an independent, largely non-commercial media sector.

The great liberal who inspired me from my days in graduate school was Alexander Meiklejohn. In the 1980s, in the United States, it was commonly argued that the First Amendment was an ahistorical commandment whereby commercial media were protected from any government regulation, except in broadcasting, regardless of the content that these media firms produced. Meiklejohn challenged that perspective and skewered it:

> First, let it be noted that, by those words [the text of the First Amendment], Congress is not debarred from all action upon freedom of speech. Legislation which abridges that freedom is forbidden, but not legislation to enlarge and enrich it. The freedom of mind

which befits members of a self-governing society is not a given and fixed part of human nature. It can be increased and established by learning, by teaching, by the unhindered flow of accurate information, by giving men health and vigor and security, by bringing them together in activities of communication and mutual understanding. And the federal legislature is not forbidden to engage in that positive enterprise of cultivating the general intelligence upon which the success of self-government so obviously depends. On the contrary, in that positive field the Congress of the United States has a heavy and basic responsibility to promote the freedom of speech.[2]

Meiklejohn opened up a new, progressive way to envision the First Amendment as a policy prescription for a self-governing society, not as protective legislation for investors in communication industries. The First Amendment is not meant to sanctify the marketplace of ideas, it is meant to ensure to every citizen 'the fullest possible participation' in the working through of social problems. As he wrote:

When a free man is voting, it is not enough that the truth is known by someone else, by some scholar or administrator or legislator. The voters must have it, all of them. The primary purpose of the First Amendment is, then, that all the citizens shall, so far as possible, understand the issues which bear upon our common life. That is why no idea, no opinion, no doubt, no belief, no counterbelief, no relevant information, may be kept from them.[3]

Meiklejohn was highly sceptical toward the commercialization of the press, and was opposed to commercial broadcasting in the 1930s. He highlighted the tension between the need for a press system to draw citizens into public life as informed participants and a press system set-up to maximize profit for investors. His thinking pointed toward radical solutions, and, in some ways, became impractical in a world where nearly all of media was conducted for profit. But it inspired me, and others, to think big, and to fight for an understanding of the First Amendment and freedom of the press that served self-government first and foremost.

The line from Meiklejohn, the classical liberal, to the socialist/Marxist Raymond Williams[4] was short and direct. When one reads Williams's classic works from the 1960s on how media industries should be structured in democratic and socialist societies, it is all but interchangeable with Meiklejohn, even if they come at it from different directions.

For that reason, I have looked at the glass of liberalism and seen it as half full. If we are ever going to change our societies for the better, it will be as advocates of the best of the liberal tradition.

Notes

1. C. B. Macpherson, *The Life and Times of Liberal Democracy* (Oxford: Oxford University Press, 1977).

2. Alexander Meiklejohn, *Political Freedom: The Constitutional Powers of the People* (New York: Harper, 1960), 16–17.

3. Ibid., 88–89.

4. Raymond Williams, "The Existing Alternatives in Communications," *Monthly Review* 65, no. 3 (2013): 92–106.

16

Liberal Legacies and Media
Reform after Neoliberalism

Jonathan Hardy

Of the values liberalism has bestowed on media, plurality ranks high. Yet to address the failures of both liberal and neoliberal approaches to media plurality we need the insights of the radical tradition.

In the West, the governing values forming twentieth-century communications were liberal, albeit split into its libertarian, private-property-protecting forms, and more interventionist, social market variants. Modern liberalism supported measures to ensure public value, from obligations on private trustees of the airwaves in the United States, to public service media, and measures to safeguard political and, later, cultural diversity, ranging from press subsidies to ownership controls. Over the last four decades neoliberalism has become the dominant value system, favouring 'deregulation' and free markets, although it has not supplanted entirely the justifications for positive intervention for social and cultural ends, or indeed allowed free market rhetoric to hamper statist action on behalf of capital control, and social control. Liberalism has been displaced, but challenging neoliberalism requires acting upon radical critiques.

Liberalism values a plural media but, in general, has wished the ends while restricting the means. Classic liberalism made the values of free speech conditional on private media ownership. Twentieth-century liberalism remained troubled by state intervention in media markets, yet, grappling with corporate combinations and commercialism, built a case for states to use the wealth of government and the rule of law to support public service media, subsidies, and obligations on private providers. Accompanying social welfare policies and the socialisation of rights, there have been demands for the providers of communication services to serve society as a whole, justifying action to tackle ownership and regulate services. But on the whole, liberalism has favoured non-intervention to protect press freedom, while its more technical justifications for public service media are widely regarded as having lost salience in a putative digital marketplace of ideas. Neoliberalism fused the various grounds for non-intervention with a more strident form of re-regulation that favoured commercial market actors and attacked public interest regulation as impeding innovation, outdated, and paternalist. Liberal approaches are still embedded in institutional and governance arrangements but face a variety of crises of effectiveness, reach, and legitimacy across media systems.

The radical tradition has tended to make three key critiques of liberal media policies. Firstly, the free press model makes liberal values contingent on privately owned and controlled media. Second, liberalism discounts the structural imbalances of power in capitalist media systems that amplify the voices and interests of elites, dominant capital interests and pro-system values through corporate ownership and control, marketers' influence, a reliance on official sources and resource-rich public relations, and the selection, management, and socialisation of media professionals. It is not only state actors who implement censorship: the market too serves to censor and organise speech rights. Third, plurality needs to extend to groups and interests marginalised within prevailing systems and cultures—which requires more thoroughgoing intervention than liberalism generally sanctions. Recent studies have highlighted the marginalisation of women in film-making,[1] of BAME workers in the creative industries,[2] and of limited working class access to industries that continue to shred the employment rights gained through unionisation and anti-discrimination efforts.[3]

Reform agendas need to identify the problems to be tackled and the scope for action. This varies considerably across, and within, media systems, where the state-party-market tripartite relationship ranges from neoliberal light touch, to social market, to market authoritarian and statist. Building policies and wider support for reform also requires understanding how neoliberalism infuses communications, not just via regulations but also through content, services, and behaviour in communications environments. We need to know how neoliberalism is 'articulated,' to use Stuart Hall's[4] resonant attempt to think through linkages without sacrificing complexity for determinism.

Take Channel 5 in the United Kingdom as an illustration. At the governance level, Channel 5 is the result of 1990s liberalisation, constrained within a progressively weakening public service framework. At the corporate level Channel 5's £450 million sale to Viacom in 2014 shifted control to a US-based, top-tier global media firm, from national capital, Richard Desmond's Northern & Shell, which owns four UK newspapers including the *Daily Express* and *Daily Star*, the *Irish Daily Star* (jointly owned with the Irish Independent Group), celebrity/ consumer magazines including *OK* magazine, and television services, amongst other holdings. The drive for profitability that is integral to this capitalist media model has more complex articulation in the particularities of Desmond's management, mixing cost-cutting with cross-promotion, chasing a commercially successful, celebrity-laden entertainment formula and enthusiastically integrating ad-financed shows and product placement into Channel 5's suite of channels before their sale to Viacom (itself heavily involved in integrating brands into its own and others' content through subsidiaries such as Viacom Velocity). But the other side of Desmond's corporate neoliberalism is the advancement of a small state, anti-welfare, and anti-immigration agenda, sustained in the *Express* and *Star*, and introduced into Desmond-owned Channel 5 through such poverty porn productions as *Benefits Britain*, and *Gypsies on Benefits and Proud*. One schools trainer, Rhiannon Colvin of MyBnk, noted of the children she teaches that 'when you ask them what the government spends its money on you'd think that the first thing they would say is schools or hospitals but they say people who are not working. Those media messages filter down.'[5] Former *Star* journalist Richard Peppiat[6] dramatically revealed how the paper's managers routinely enforced a narrow, derogatory framing of Muslims, while its reactionary stance on issues including race, immigration, sexualities, and feminism have drawn widespread criticism. The problems of media ownership and control that troubled early twentieth-century liberalism are all present, and will not be tackled simply by swapping corporate owners.

More broadly, there are complex patterns of corporate convergence and de-convergence, yet concentration of media ownership remains a persistent feature and pervasive critical issue. In the United Kingdom, three companies hold 71 per cent share of the national newspaper market, while just five companies command 80 per cent share of the combined print and digital audience.[7] Google, now the world's largest media company by revenue, accounted for 49 per cent of Internet advertising revenue worldwide in December 2012.[8] Google was expected to have 55 per cent of global search advertising spending in 2015.[9] Apple's iTunes, YouTube's videos, and Facebook's social networking traffic dominate their respective markets in the United States, United Kingdom, and elsewhere. Networked communications have transformed the capacity for messages to be created and exchanged, yet problems of scarcity and control remain evident. It would be wrong to conclude that the massively increased availability of digital content itself diminishes concern about the sources and supply of news, controls over access to films or sports, or the multiplatform share and reach of large media companies.

Beginning in the late twentieth century, James Curran,[10] Edwin Baker,[11] and others advanced the case for a plural media system, with a public service media core and various surrounding sectors: commercial, civic, social market, and professional. This blended liberal concerns about the need for protection against statist power, with radical democratic attention to corporate power. It sought to incorporate the many communication jobs required of a media system: self-constitution as well as sharing, antagonism as well as consensus building. It combined a multidimensional assessment of state and market with an appreciation that the different purposes required in turn a mix of forms of organisation and finance, generating different communication spaces and styles. Such normative models were constructed to address problems in Anglo-American media systems, and while their authors would reject universalising them, these systems also need to be revised and refreshed beyond their mass media presumptions in order to assist reformers in communications environments today, as I argue in *Critical Political Economy of the Media*.[12]

Working on UK media plurality issues for the Campaign for Press and Broadcasting Freedom, I have contributed to proposals that would set limits on the maximum market share of private enterprises but which are guided by a broader principle: for media that serve public audiences, with size and reach come responsibilities. Private providers with significant market share should meet requirements and obligations to safeguard our communication rights. Above caps set for total market share by companies operating in key media markets, or when democratically responsive regulation demands it, communication services should be provided by public trusts or similar non-profit, publicly accountable arrangements, not by commercial providers.[13]

Radical reform is required. Liberalism's presumption that commercial media could safeguard citizens against the state has not travelled well across two centuries. From Putin's market authoritarianism, to the US military-media complex integrating telecoms, media, and Internet giants in mass surveillance, state and market can become fatefully entwined. We have had authoritarian, paternal, and commercial media systems, and it is surely time, as Raymond Williams[14] suggested, to try the democratic one.

The radical tradition's critique of market control is also needed to address two key challenges for liberalism that arise from emergent communications systems. First, declining advertising subsidy undermines the resources for the news and information required for self-government and liberty. The revenue base for non-commercial content is shrinking while the various market interventions liberalism advanced are either declining or unstable, from public service media to news media subsidies. Second, the commercial media solution is to grant marketers ever greater influence over content, as both embrace camouflaged advertising in the form of paid, sponsored, and branded content, native ads and the shared pursuit of content marketing.

Here, the repertoire of responses from liberalism are contradictory and insufficient. Historically, advertising support has been broadly welcomed as underpinning media independence from political interference, leaving the threat to media independence from marketers' influence relatively disarticulated. Meanwhile, the championing of free speech has been adopted by advertisers claiming the right to advertise. The principle of separation of media and advertising has been eroded in European broadcasting, while publishers stress test tolerance for marketer-funded content amongst readers, staff, and other publics. In the United States, the Federal Trade Commission's (FTC) regulation of native advertising focuses on preventing consumer deception, reaffirming 'the principle that advertising and promotional messages should be identifiable as advertising' to consumers.[15] Yet, the FTC is not concerned about the impact of branded content on the quality and integrity of media channels. Consumers only need to be informed that articles are sponsored when the sponsor's brand is promoted. Once we are past the hurdle of consumer recognition of native ads, there is little left in this prevailing regulatory arsenal to support restrictions. Paradoxically, liberalism's conceptualisation of media freedom has contributed to these conditions for inaction, and yet retains powerful justifications for action. Liberalism's emphasis on protecting communications for civic purposes must inform a new movement to counter the weakening of media bulwarks against marketing logics.

Liberalism is needed for at least two main reasons. The first is that the values for communications that arise from the complex confluence of liberal thinking, include promoting conditions for mutual exchanges of a plurality of information, ideas, and imagery to safeguard democratic rule, strengthen social understanding and cooperation, and enrich cultural life. The second is that reforming media systems, such as that of the United Kingdom, will require a coalition as broad as that of Chartism two centuries ago. Liberals and radicals need to work together, because doing so enhances both the goals of and the steps towards communications reform.

Notes

1. Stephen Follows, *Gender within Film Crews*, 2014, accessed February 20, 2016, http://stephenfollows.com/reports/Gender_Within_Film_Crews -stephenfollows_com.pdf.
2. Creative Skillset, *Employment Census of the Creative Media Industries*, 2012, accessed February 20, 2016, http://creativeskillset.org/about_us/publications.
3. Doris Ruth Eikhof and Chris Warhurst, "The Promised Land? Why Social Inequalities Are Systemic in the Creative Industries," *Employee Relations* 35, no. 5 (2013): 495–508. doi:10.1108/ER-08-2012-0061.
4. Stuart Hall and Lawrence Grossberg, "On Postmodernism and Articulation: An Interview with Stuart Hall," *Journal of Communication Inquiry* 10, no. 2 (1986): 45–60. doi:10.1177/019685998601000204.
5. Katie Allen, "Lessons in Finance: Schoolchildren Taught the Value of Everything," *Guardian*, July 22, 2014, accessed February 22, 2016, http://www .theguardian.com/business/2014/jul/22/lessons-in-finance-british -schoolchildren.

6. Richard Peppiatt, "Richard Peppiatt's Letter to *Daily Star* Proprietor Richard Desmond," *Guardian*, March 4, 2011, accessed February 22, 2016, http://www .theguardian.com/media/2011/mar/04/daily-star-reporter-letter-full?guni= Article:in%20body%20link.

7. Media Reform Coalition, *Who Owns the UK Media?*, 2015, accessed February 22, 2016, http://www.mediareform.org.uk/who-owns-the-uk-media.

8. Zenith Optimedia, "Google Takes Top Position in Global Media Owner Rankings," May 28, 2013, accessed February 22, 2016, http://www .zenithoptimedia.com/wp-content/uploads/2013/05/Top-30-Global-Media -Owners-2013-press-release.pdf.

9. eMarketer, "Google Will Take 55% of Search Ad Dollars Globally in 2015: Baidu is Next-largest with 8.8% Share of the $81.59 Billion Market," March 31, 2015, accessed February 22, 2016, http://www.emarketer.com/Article/Google -Will-Take-55-of-Search-Ad-Dollars-Globally-2015/1012294.

10. James Curran, *Media and Power* (London: Routledge, 2002).

11. C. Edwin Baker, *Media, Markets, and Democracy* (Cambridge: Cambridge University Press, 2002).

12. Jonathan Hardy, *Critical Political Economy of the Media: An Introduction* (Abingdon, UK: Routledge, 2014).

13. CPBF, "Submission by the Campaign for Press and Broadcasting Freedom to the Culture, Media and Sport Committee Inquiry into Media Pluralism," January 18, 2012, accessed 22 February, 2016, http://www.cpbf.org.uk/body .php?subject=media%20ownership&doctype=campaigns&id=2916.

14. Raymond Williams, *Communications* (London: Penguin, 1962).

15. Federal Trade Commission, "Enforcement Policy Statement on Deceptively Formatted Advertisements," December 22, 2015, accessed 22 February, 2016, https://www.ftc.gov/system/files/documents/public_statements/896923/151 222deceptiveenforcement.pdf.

17

Liberal Reform and Normativity in Media Analysis

John Steel

The relationship between liberal democracy and media freedom is of course fundamental to the democratic well-being of societies. To state the contrary is to court controversy and possible ridicule. Yet amongst the sections of the Left and those who might be termed social liberals or progressives, the entanglement of socially progressive liberal ideals and aspirations with economic liberalism and its material consequences has hitherto been fraught with challenges. As Julian Petley,[1] John Keane,[2] and many others have observed, economic freedom is generally applied to conceptions of media freedom to the detriment of democratic culture. Those defending economic liberalism argue that in order to have a truly free press, societies must have an unconstrained economic media environment. These tensions between social liberals and economic liberals are longstanding and show little sign of being resolved in these neoliberal times.

My main argument, developed more fully elsewhere,[3] is oriented towards two particular interrelated areas of debate within media and, more specifically, journalism studies that I think are pertinent to questions of the relationship between liberalism and the media. The first relates to media structures and particularly to the debate about media reform. The second concerns the growth of work on role perceptions of journalists and media workers.

The first part of my argument addresses what I will call structural normativity in media analysis. What I'm interested in here are the often implicit normative claims that are made in areas of media scholarship that relate to so-called 'media systems', media structures, and the political economy of the media. In sum my argument is that the basis of the normative claims that are ostensibly rooted in liberal political theory—claims that are generally made about the role and functions of journalism in contemporary society—are lacking in critical rigour as they are too firmly embedded in outmoded conceptions of democracy and democratic theory. Such analyses, I suggest, are dependent upon a decrepit conception of political culture and liberal democratic participation that sees media and journalism as facilitators of democratic politics and plurality, yet which are unable to deliver on the promise of democratic freedom because journalism and the media more broadly are stifled by the priority of profit. Generally, debates about the need for greater media plurality, accountability, and representation are articulated in order to challenge, or at least highlight, the commercial imperatives of large media corporations and stress the democratic deficit that contemporary business models of journalism promote. If we look to how this work filters through into the realm of journalism and media policy, we see it most starkly in the United Kingdom in the work of campaign groups like the Media Reform Coalition, the Campaign for Press and

Broadcasting Freedom, and Hacked Off. These groups provide important critical spaces and pressure points that highlight where the commercial imperatives of media organisations, which stifle democratic deliberation and representation, are confronted. Such groups of course gain intellectual substance from a long tradition of critical scholarship into media systems, structures, and processes. However, I suggest that the central problem of such groups, and of some of the intellectual currents that they draw from, lies in their aspirations to reform media policy in ways that aspire to the cultivation of a more accountable, representative, and diverse media environment. Yet within the confines of neoliberalism, such calls for reform seem harder to attain then ever. What do these terms actually mean within this neoliberal era, given the prevailing liberal orthodoxy? I contend that such claims, though laudable, are often made without sufficient critical engagement with normative foundations; or without providing a sufficiently clear notion of how reform might stimulate/cultivate enhanced political participation and political culture; or, more importantly, without considering what such a reinvigorated political culture might look like given the current context of neoliberalism.

This brings me to the second part of my argument. The work on role perceptions within journalism studies is something that has seen significant development in recent years. This research builds on the work of Wolfgang Donsbach[4] and examines the lived experiences, perceptions, and motivations of those working within the journalism and media industries. It is orientated towards understanding how media workers and journalists see their roles. Again, such lived experiences are often articulated or framed in relation to a set of general normative claims concerning democracy and the deliberative power of journalism and media systems. In this work we see a tendency to offer idealised notions of journalism and its democratic functioning, within a reflective framework that highlights the contradictions and tendencies within the production of news and amongst news workers themselves. In contrast to the aforementioned structural analyses, this work draws on lived experiences and insights in order to explore issues of democratic accountability and representation from the perspective of journalists themselves.

Though offering a valuable insight into the workings and changing dynamics of journalism in different contexts, this work suffers in much the same way as the reform orientated narratives in that it has the tendency to claim implicitly or at least draw attention to the idea that democratic culture is something that requires rehabilitation *and* that the media, and journalism practice in particular, are important sites for such rehabilitation. Yet again this journalistic praxis is gauged in relation to what I would argue are a degraded set of ideals and aspirations; degraded in the sense that the grip of neoliberalism that, despite its crises, shows no signs of being challenged by new ideas and new ways of imagining democratic society. Such work is redolent of a form of identity politics in which the social construction of journalism or the journalist is seen as the central site of conflict and contestation, and thereby as the solution to the problems of journalism and its democratic deficit. Such work, however, tends to be divorced from a rigorous engagement with important concepts and debates such as, for example, the nature and character of political deliberation, the substance of political culture, or indeed the nature of contemporary democracy itself.

In sum, my argument is that we need first to reconceptualise journalism's functions and take a closer look at some of the normative claims and aspirations with which many strands of journalism and media studies research engage, and to ask the question: are the normative claims upon which such analyses of media are made in need of serious theoretical reconsideration? I would answer this question in the affirmative.

Where might we begin such a theoretical reconsideration? How might we move the discussion forward? One way to start might be by broadening our analysis, and it could be that we can then start to move towards the development of ideas towards which journalism praxis might more optimistically be oriented. Ultimately it may be that we need to start to think beyond the ideas of James Madison, John Stuart Mill, and John Dewey—all key contributors to the liberal democratic idea of press freedom—and to re-imagine conceptions of deliberation and political participation in ways that might underscore new normative foundations. Here I am mindful of the work of Jodi Dean,[5] who analyses how critical responses might emerge from within neoliberal societies yet still be critical of and possibly transcend such a context. Dean's work attempts to rehabilitate a Marxian analysis, which grapples with the complexities of contemporary capitalism in ways that offer new opportunities for understanding the very basis of democratic culture and critical politics. More specifically Dean's analysis of 'communicative capitalism' orientates us towards thinking about how neoliberalism has co-opted much of the moral capital from the reformist Left and incorporated it into its own manifestations of power and authority. She suggests that under communicative capitalism 'Right and Left share the same rhetoric of democracy, a rhetoric merging ethics and economics, discussion and competition so that each is a version of each other.'[6] Drawing on Slavoj Zizek, she demonstrates that the communicative and deliberative opportunities provided by our new communication environment are ultimately subsumed into the politics and culture of liberal individualism, and therefore limit any genuine opportunities to move outside or beyond our current predicaments. She goes on to suggest that 'the problem isn't democratisation. It is the Left's failure to think beyond democracy and defend a vision of equality and solidarity, its unwillingness to reinvent its modes of dreaming.'[7] While it remains important to counter neoliberal culture and politics and to contest neoliberalism's incursions into everyday life, we should also think hard about Dean's challenge in order to imagine new visions of politics that do not cling to decrepit notions of liberal political idealism.

Notes

1. Julian Petley, "The Leveson Inquiry: Journalism Ethics and Press Freedom," *Journalism* 13, no. 4 (2012): 529–38. doi:10.1177/1464884912443498.

2. John Keane, *The Media and Democracy* (Cambridge: Polity Press, 2004).

3. John Steel, "Reappraising Journalism's Normative Foundations," in *Rethinking Journalism Again: Societal Role and Public Relevance in a Digital Age*, eds. Chris Peters and Marcel Broersma (Abingdon, UK: Routledge 2016).

4. Wolfgang Donsbach, "Journalists' Conception of Their Roles: Comparative Indicators for the Way British and German Journalists Define Their Relations to the Public," *Gazette* 32 (1983), 19–36; Wolfgang Donsbach, "Journalists and Their Professional Identities," in *The Routledge Companion to News and Journalism*, ed. Stuart Allen (Abingdon, UK: Routledge, 2010), 38–59.

5. Jodi Dean, *Democracy and Other Neoliberal Fantasies: Communicative Capitalism and Left Politics* (Durham, NC: Duke University Press, 2009); Jodi Dean, *Blog Theory: Feedback and Capture in the Circuits of Drive* (Cambridge: Polity Press, 2010).

6. Dean, *Democracy and Other Neoliberal Fantasies*, 18.

7. Ibid., 17.

18

Liberalism, the Media, and the NHS

Colin Leys

Future historians may well look back at the passage of the 2012 Health and Social Care (HSC) Act as the pivotal moment in the conversion of England from a collectivist society framed by the post-war welfare state to an individualist society in which people are responsible for securing their own welfare, and state provision is not only minimised but also stigmatised.

By 2012 local government had long been converted from a democratic agency for providing collective services, including housing, schooling, and long-term care for the old and frail, to an administrative dependency of Whitehall, stripped of many of these functions and obliged to implement an unremitting contraction of those that remained. Universities had already been converted into a system of training institutions, through replacing state funding with loan-financed fees, which from 2010 were set at a level that made it quixotic for a student without superior family connections to regard getting a degree as anything than a means to a job.[1]

The list could easily be extended. But the attempt to convert health care from a free public service back to a commodity for sale ought to be specially remembered as symbolic of the overall transformation, because the National Health Service (NHS) serves everybody, and—to a greater extent than any other public service—makes everybody equal. This unquestioned right of access to care, regardless of your social status or social condition, is what underlies the public's refusal to stop loving the NHS, and even being willing to pay more tax to keep it. In health care alone people still are, in the Conservative Party's famously inept phrase, 'all in it together.'

Yet, following the passage of the 2012 Health and Social Care Act, a transition from the provision of care by public providers to provision by for-profit companies was pushed ahead rapidly, the scope of free services was contracting and the reintroduction of charges, long favoured by neoliberals, was again being actively canvassed (on the false pretext that there was no alternative way of closing the NHS funding gap). From start to finish the process not merely lacked an electoral mandate, but also broke an explicit pre-election promise not to undertake further top-down reform of the NHS.

There are practical obstacles in the way of completing this project. As both UnitedHealth and Serco have found, you can't make a profit out of primary care by cutting costs, because 90 per cent of patient interactions with health care are with primary care, so the public quickly sees what is happening.[2] But the large-scale outsourcing of community-based specialist services such as speech therapy, physiotherapy, and post-natal, mental health and elderly care that is currently under way is unlikely to be reversed; in these sectors the negative impact of profit-driven cost-cutting will be less universally felt and resented. It is also a fair bet that more and more NHS hospitals will be put out of business as Monitor requires specific hospital services to be 'unbundled' and contracted out to private companies. But will future historians see the Health and Social Care Act of 2012 as the same kind of watershed as the repeal of the Corn Laws of 1846, or the Trade Disputes Act of 2006? Are they any more likely to do so than editors and journalists today, who have shown little inclination to frame the act in these terms?

As Oliver Huitson and others have shown, very few newspapers, and among broadcasters only Channel 4, maintained a serious critical interest in the HSC Bill during its prolonged parliamentary passage.[3] The huge investment by the private health industry in lobbying for the bill (exposed, along with other scandals, in Tamasin Cave and Andy Rowell's study of lobbying in *A Quiet Word*);[4] the many undeclared interests in the private health industry of MPs and numerous peers; the central role accorded to the global consultants McKinsey and KPMG in drafting legislation that promoted their business clients' interests; the manifest untruth of the government's claim, stated in the preamble to the bill, that its aim was to empower GPs—little if any of this was consistently commented on. Nor was there much appraisal of the opposition case advanced by a growing segment of the medical profession. The government cited the support for the bill of, in particular, certain active pro-market GPs (notably in the National Association of Primary Care and The NHS Alliance), but their history and commercial interests were rarely noted.

The point of all this is not to reproach either print journalists or broadcasters but to ask why most of the media failed so comprehensively not only to provide a critical account of the aims of the bill and the forces behind it, the flawed legislative process, and so on, but also any 'external' critique, framing this measure in its historical context and pointing out what it meant for English society.

It is no doubt a major oversimplification, but from the standpoint of anyone engaged in the effort to defend the NHS, the explanation appears over-determined. Most newspaper owners support business and competition. Even the *Guardian*, which supported the Liberal Democrats in the 2010 general election, did not oppose the Health and Social Care Bill unequivocally, or highlight the way in which Shirley Williams, the Lib. Dem.'s 'national treasure' and self-styled defender of the NHS, enabled the bill's passage in the Upper House. In addition almost all papers are losing money and cutting editorial staff, so journalists have no time to do investigative work, or even double-source, and have little option but to use government press releases for an estimated 80 per cent of their output (as revealed by Nick Davies in *Flat Earth News*), even when they know that these releases—and not least the Department of Health's—are often shamelessly spun.[5]

Less predictable was the way in which the BBC failed in its task of public education on the bill, especially by including virtually none of the bill's best-informed critics in broadcast debates. Again, there seems to be a superabundance of causes, from the Corporation's bruising conflict with the Labour government over the David Kelly 'dodgy dossier' affair to the ongoing fear of cuts to the licence fee, of being required to share it with competing broadcasters, and of being subject to increased regulation by Ofcom.

And this kind of fear links the reticence of the BBC to that of both the medical profession and university-based health policy researchers. Once NHS hospitals became trusts, paid on the basis of patient throughput and being obliged to compete for patients, it was inevitable that, like any other business, they would require their staff to avoid public criticism, not only of their own particular hospital but also of government policy. The independence of medical professional bodies has also been increasingly circumscribed and the British Medical Association (BMA) leadership, traditionally and understandably anxious not to find itself at odds with the government, did not seriously oppose the bill and could not be looked to by doctors opposed to the measure for much support.[6] As for health policy experts, academic careers now depend on publishing and on securing funding for research, and the Department of Health is the major source of funding for research in health policy as well as in medicine. Outspoken criticism of the bill carried a risk that many health policy researchers were not willing to take.

In short there was a comprehensive alignment of incentives to conform that embraced not just the media but most of the active participants in the story too. And perhaps more important than anything else, in the long run, is the difficulty of continuing to see as objectionable something that has become accepted by everyone around you as at least inevitable, if not positively reasonable and satisfactory. This is most obvious in the case of the BBC: defining its commitment to political impartiality in terms of standing midway between the views of the major parties now means standing near the middle of a neoliberal consensus, one which has been internalised by its staff. What would have been a mainstream critical standpoint thirty or even twenty years ago gradually came to be seen as eccentric, marginal, unrealistic, political, ideological, and so on. But the same process is at work everywhere, to a greater or lesser extent. In the Department of Health, in the NHS, and in the commentariat, the post-war political culture—in which social democracy, conservatism, liberalism, and even communism were all in contest—has been increasingly replaced by a single neoliberal culture. Reinforced by lobbying and spin, and enforced by sanctions, it has become increasingly naturalised.

How profoundly this hegemony has penetrated the media was dramatically illustrated by the failure to predict the victory of Jeremy Corbyn in the Labour Party leadership election of 2015—or to come to terms with it afterwards. The swelling current of hostility to neoliberalism and its social effects caught the commentariat by surprise: it had given up thinking that there were any legitimate alternative ideas. As Paul Myerscough recorded in the *London Review of Books* in October 2015, even the 'liberal' *Guardian* found it difficult to treat Corbyn as a legitimate leader despite his large majority, while his election 'dislocated' the BBC's notion of what constitutes impartiality—itself a profoundly liberal commitment:

> Because its notion of political balance between left and right is defined by the Labour and Conservative Parties, its spectrum of opinion has narrowed and its fulcrum drifted to the right in concert with New Labour. Corbyn has reopened the gap, but the BBC has not adjusted. ... Its norm remains a "balance" between the Tories and the Labour right. By defining himself against the establishment, Corbyn becomes an outsider, an insurgent. ... irrevocably other.[7]

What all this shows is that neoliberalism leaves little room for palaeoliberalism—political liberalism in the original meaning of the term. Palaeoliberalism was a product of the early years of capitalism, when supporters of freedom saw private property as a counter to political absolutism, and thought that economic freedom and political freedom went hand in hand. Neoliberalism, in contrast, asserts the supremacy of economic freedom untrammelled by politics—that is, a new absolutism, the absolutism of market value. Liberals can no longer champion political freedom if it runs counter to the precepts of this new, triumphant doctrine of economic freedom, according to which no policy is legitimate that is not the result of market forces.[8]

The fate of the NHS at the hands of the liberal media in 2012 and since is an example of the consequences. They wring their hands over the detail of the ongoing fragmentation, financial starvation, and calculated mismanagement of the NHS. But they cannot bring themselves to acknowledge the full import of the neoliberals' plans for the NHS, or the immensity of the social regression that completion of these plans will entail.

Notes

1. BBC News, "Tuition Fees Vote: Plans Approved Despite Rebellion," December 9, 2010, accessed February 22, 2016, http://www.bbc.co.uk/news/uk-politics-11952449.
2. On Serco see NHS Support Federation, http://www.nhsforsale.info/private-providers/private-provider-profiles-2/serco.html; on UnitedHealth see Gareth Iacobucci, "UnitedHealth Quits Primary Care and Sells Off Surgeries to the Practice," Pulse, April 20, 2011, http://www.pulsetoday.co.uk/unitedhealth-quits-primary-care-and-sells-off-surgeries-to-the-practice/12199561. fullarticle.
3. Oliver Huitson, "Hidden in Plain Sight," in *NHS SOS: How The NHS Was Betrayed—And How We Can Save It*, eds. Raymond Tallis and Jacky Davis, (Oxford: Oneworld Publications 2013), pp. 150–73.
4. Tamasin Cave and Andy Rowell, *A Quiet Word: Lobbying, Crony Capitalism and Broken Politics in Britain* (London: The Bodley Head, 2013).

5. Nick Davies, *Flat Earth News: An Award-Winning Reporter Exposes Falsehood, Distortion and Propaganda in the Global Media* (London: Chatto 2008).
6. On the BMA see Jacky Davis and David Wrigley, "The Silence of the Lambs," in *NHS SOS: How the NHS Was Betrayed—And How We Can Save It,* eds. Raymond Tallis and Jacky Davis, (Oxford: Oneworld Publications 2013), pp. 88–120.
7. Paul Myerscough, "Corbyn in the Media," *London Review of Books* 37, no. 20 (2015): 8–9.
8. For a trenchant exposition of this reality see Colin Crouch, *The Knowledge Corrupters: Hidden Consequences of the Financial Takeover of Public Life* (Cambridge: Polity Press, 2016).

19

Charlie Hebdo Tragedy: Free Speech and Its Broader Contexts

Des Freedman

The horrific killing of ten journalists and two policemen in Paris in January 2015 has been widely described in the mainstream media as a 'murderous attack on Western freedoms,'[1] notably freedom of expression and the right to satirise. In response, certain bloggers have insisted that the 'attack [had] nothing to do with free speech'[2] but was simply part of the ongoing war between Western governments and jihadists.

The reality is that the killers *did* single out journalists and timed their attack to coincide with the weekly editorial meeting at *Charlie Hebdo* in order to secure maximum impact. The cartoonists now join the growing number of journalists killed 'in the line of duty'. The Committee to Protect Journalists estimates that nearly twelve hundred journalists have been killed in the last twenty-five years (with sixty killed in 2014 alone).[3] These numbers include not simply the high-profile murders of reporters by ISIS in Syria but also cases like the seventeen Palestinian journalists killed by the Israeli army in Gaza[4] together with the sixteen reporters killed by US military fire in Iraq.[5] Strangely enough, these latter killings do not seem to have generated the same claims from leading commentators that they constituted a 'murderous attack on Western freedoms.' Yet the fact remains that it is an outrage—whatever the identity of the assailant or the victim—that a single journalist should have lost their life simply for covering or commenting on a conflict.

But let's be clear: what happened at *Charlie Hebdo* was not an assault on some generalised notion of press freedom but an attack on a specific news outlet that has regularly and proudly featured offensive images of Muslims (including publication of the hugely controversial Danish cartoons in 2006). The killings are likely to have been motivated not by a dislike of images per se but by the foreign policy dynamics of France and other Western states. The target, in other words, wasn't an *idea* but, in the eyes of the gunmen, representatives of the forces with whom they are in conflict. So this wasn't about some kind of Islamic opposition to satire or free speech, or evidence of some genetic flaw that results in the lack of a sense of humour, but a violent act designed to spark a reaction—of increased anti-terror laws, of more surveillance, of more anti-Muslim racism—that will fuel the tiny ranks of jihad. It was, as Juan Cole argues, 'a strategic strike, aiming at polarizing the French and European public.'[6]

Those commentators peddling the argument that the shootings were all about a 'medieval'[7] determination to stifle free speech and undermine our free media have sought to marginalise the wider political context as if there are no consequences for the West of interventions in Iraq, Syria, and Afghanistan let alone the situation in Palestine. In their obsession with the sanctity of freedom of expression, they seek to bury the notion that there might be blowback as a result of Western occupation and intervention along the lines predicted by the former head of MI5, Eliza Manningham-Buller, when she talked about how 'our involvement in Iraq radicalised a few among a generation of young people who saw [it] as an attack on Islam.'[8]

But of course it is far more convenient to adopt a 'clash of civilisations' thesis and to shunt aside uncomfortable geopolitical realities for the more soothing talk of free speech and absolutist speech rights. Yet even the liberal conception of free speech wasn't designed to mean the freedom of the powerful to insult the powerless but precisely the opposite: to make sure that there could be a check on the most powerful groups in society and to protect the speech rights of minorities.

For some, however, free speech seems to be interpreted as the right to bully, to mock, and to stereotype without regard for the consequences. Satire—all satire no matter the content or the target—is now to be treated as a basic hallmark of democracy. In this context, Will Self's reaction to the *Charlie Hebdo* tragedy is instructive:

> The test I apply to something to see whether it truly is satire derives from H. L. Mencken's definition of good journalism: It should 'afflict the comfortable and comfort the afflicted.' The trouble with a lot of so-called 'satire' directed against religiously motivated extremists is that it's not clear who it's afflicting, or who it's comforting.[9]

In the days that followed the *Charlie Hebdo* shootings, the barometer of freedom of expression for many liberals increasingly seemed to be about whether you're brave enough to publish material that you know is offensive to millions of people. Nick Cohen, for example, returned from a vigil in Trafalgar Square not calling for unity and peace but hoping that 'tomorrow's papers and news programmes will prove their commitment to freedom by republishing the *Charlie Hebdo* cartoons.'[10] David Aaronovitch then used the freedom afforded by his column in the *Times* to warn those people who don't share his view of liberal tolerance that they should leave the country if they're offended by the publication of the cartoons: 'You live here, that's what you agree to. You don't like it, go somewhere else.'[11] But what kind of freedom is it that is measured by its ability to offend and not to enlighten, and characterised by an underlying threat that if you don't like 'my kind of freedom' then you're not free to live with me?

Many muscular liberal commentators like Cohen and Aaronovitch took to the airwaves in response to the Paris outrage to argue that political correctness and a widespread cowardice have taken grip, with the result that too many media outlets are now self-censoring and are too nervous to circulate controversial material. But there is nothing brave about large and powerful media institutions reproducing these images. The real reason why the vast majority of the British media has, thus far, chosen *not* to publish the cartoons is because there is a perception that publication would cause unnecessary harm and fan the flames of a situation that needs calming. By and large, that position continued to hold following what happened at *Charlie Hebdo* in spite of Aaronovitch's call for the press to show just how brave they are. A genuinely free media, on the other hand, would devote their resources to reporting on and monitoring power, to thinking about solutions to the problems we face, and to find ways to mark their independence that are not about sensationalism and cheap headlines.

In so much of the media coverage following the attacks, a horrific crime was distorted to fit the prism of commentators fixated on a crude and absolutist fetish of free speech. Its real context—an asymmetrical and violent war on terror—was essentially stripped from the scene. This wasn't an attack on humour or on the Western concept of freedom but an outrage designed to produce precisely the reaction of division and hatred that we should be doing everything we can to resist.[12]

Notes

1. *Daily Mail Comment*, "A Murderous Attack on Western Freedoms," January 7, 2015, accessed March 7, 2016, http://www.dailymail.co.uk/debate/article -2901368/DAILY-MAIL-COMMENT-murderous-attack-Western-freedoms.html.
2. Asghar Bukhari, "*Charlie Hebdo*: This Attack Was Nothing to Do with Free Speech—It Was about War," January 7, 2015, accessed March 7, 2016, https:// medium.com/@asgharbukhari/charlie-hebdo-this-attack-was-nothing-to -do-with-free-speech-it-was-about-war-26aff1c3e998#.28wgl12fm.
3. Data from the Committee to Protect Journalists, https://cpj.org/killed, accessed March 7, 2016.
4. Counter Current News admin., "These 17 Journalists Were Killed by Israel in Gaza," Counter Current News, August 29, 2014, accessed March 7, 2016, http:// countercurrentnews.com/2014/08/these-17-journalists-were-killed-by-israel -in-gaza.
5. Ann Scott Tyson, "Military's Killing of 2 Journalists in Iraq Detailed in New Book," *Washington Post*, September 15, 2009, accessed March 7, 2016, http:// www.washingtonpost.com/wp-dyn/content/article/2009/09/14/ AR2009091403262.html.
6. Juan Cole, "Sharpening Contradictions: Why al-Qaeda Attacked Satirists in Paris," Informed Comment, January 7, 2015, accessed March 7, 2016, http:// www.juancole.com/2015/01/sharpening-contradictions-satirists.html.
7. *Daily Mail Comment*, "A Murderous Attack".
8. Richard Norton-Taylor, "Iraq Inquiry: Eliza Manningham-Buller's Devastating Testimony," *Guardian*, July 20, 2010, accessed March 7, 2016, http://www.theguardian.com/uk/2010/jul/20/iraq-inquiry-eliza -manningham-buller.

9. Will Self quoted in *Vice*, "Europe's Leading Satirists Respond to the 'Charlie Hebdo' Massacre", January 7, 2015, accessed March 7, 2016, http://www.vice .com/read/satirists-respond-to-charlie-hebdo-shooting-876.

10. Nick Cohen, "*Charlie Hebdo*: The Truths That Ought to Be Self-evident But Still Aren't," *Spectator*, January 8, 2015, accessed March 7, 2016, http://blogs .spectator.co.uk/2015/01/charlie-hebdo-the-truths-that-ought-to-be-self -evident-but-still-arent.

11. David Aaronovitch, "Our Cowardice Helped to Allow This Attack," *Times,* January 8, 2015, accessed March 7, 2016, http://www.thetimes.co.uk/tto/ opinion/columnists/article4316868.ece.

12. AFP, "Paris Shooting Triggers Attacks on Muslim Targets," *Al Arabiya English*, January 8, 2015, accessed March 7, 2016, http://english.alarabiya.net/en/ News/world/2015/01/08/Bomb-blast-near-mosque-in-northern-France-.html.

20

Latin American Media and the Shortcomings of Liberalism

Alejandro Abraham-Hamanoiel

One of the strongest appeals of liberalism as a political doctrine is its supposed universality. Although writing in particular socio-political circumstances, the first European liberals championed equality and liberty as universal principles and declared the right to property and free trade, alongside religious liberty and press freedom, to be fundamental human prerogatives. These ideas greatly inspired the Latin American Wars of Independence fought throughout the nineteenth century. These revolutions saw the establishment of a dozen new republics and their adoption of liberal-inspired constitutions. Since then freedom of expression has been, at least nominally, legally guaranteed in all Latin American countries and has been portrayed as a method to ensure individual liberty in the face of state power.

However, the classic understanding of freedom of expression as the absence of all legal constraints to publish an idea or publicly express an opinion has never been enough to protect this right. On the one hand, newspaper owners in the nineteenth century, as media impresarios went on to do in the twentieth, more often than not sided with repressive regimes to silence individual voices in the region.[1] Eventually, at the dawn of broadcasting technologies, freedom of expression would be translated by Latin American governments as an unregulated media market in which the state refrained from owning and operating radio and television stations but kept a rigid control on what could be broadcast by commercial providers. On the other hand, the liberal protection of an individual right to expression did not envision the emergence of large media corporations, whose commercial interests would outweigh their democratic responsibilities.

Concentration of media power has long been a historical reality in Latin America. By the end of the twentieth century the monopolization of national media markets by large corporations became as big a danger to free speech as the direct censorship exercised by the state. As a result of a narrow understanding of freedom of expression and a lack of political will, the diversity of voices within the media systems of the region stalled; instead of reducing the historical influence of media moguls, the electoral reforms that during the 1990s transformed the region and restored multiparty democracy, granted these corporations a new hold on the political parties.

In Mexico, perhaps the Latin American country that most passionately adopted the neoliberal agenda and one in which media concentration has reached one of the highest levels in the world,[2] the limits of the classic liberal conception of freedom of expression can be better perceived by analysing who exploits, and more importantly who cannot exploit, the national airwaves. In addition to the unsurmountable entry barrier present in a market in which two family-owned corporations control over 90 per cent of all television stations and ten groups own 70 per cent of all radio[3], media democratization in Mexico is obstructed by the legal near impossibility of setting up non-profit, community based stations. It is important to mention that in Mexico, like in most other Latin American countries, the airwaves are inalienable resources that the state administers in the name of all citizens.

Notwithstanding recent media reforms, which rather than opening opportunities to local voices has allowed foreign investment into the audiovisual market,[4] a non-commercial, community based media has yet to be fully recognized by the state. Since the early 2000s, the Mexican branch of the World Association of Community Radio Broadcasting (AMARC), has maintained a long-running campaign to push for the legal recognition of community broadcasting as an alternative to commercial media. It has also given legal and financial advice to a number of community radios already operating in the country. These stations, which are often situated on marginalized areas serving segregated minorities, do not only lack government support and full legal recognition but are often prosecuted. According to a special report by the Inter-American Court of Human Rights,[5] aggression against community broadcasters by state officials is a reality in the country. AMARC Mexico has documented[6] these attacks, which are designed to intimidate and are often disproportionate and violent. For example, in 2009 the community radio Tierra y Libertad, with less than forty watts of power, serving a small working-class neighbourhood in the city of Monterrey and staffed by less than a dozen volunteers, was raided by over a hundred police officers; Hector Caméro, its director and founder, was originally sentenced to two years in prison for the unlawful exploitation of a national asset and he is still fighting in the courts. Tragically, community broadcasters are also part of the increasing number of journal-ists being killed in the country.[7]

Critics could argue that a truly liberal media policy would not prohibit community media and would instead allow the airwaves to become an open market. This approach, even if efficiently enacted by the state, would never do enough to protect and promote freedom of expression for all members of society. Liberal theory is ill-equipped to deal with existing and historic inequalities; the market alone would never be enough to dismantle the media monopolies that plague Latin American media. Competing on a hypothetical level playing field would do little to diversify the media environment after decades in which urban minorities, indigenous communities, and rural inhabitants have been prevented from broadcasting their hopes and opinions.

In recent years, a number of Latin American countries have begun to challenge the media corporations dominating their markets and have embarked upon systematic processes of media reform.[8] These changes to legislation have often been decried by liberal commentators as populist attacks on freedom of expression. These reforms have nevertheless gen-erated new opportunities for communities and individuals to fully exercise their right to public expression, often for the first time. For example, in 2009 the Argentinian government de-termined that one-third of its airwaves should be reserved for non-profit organizations,[9] a law that has encouraged the devel-opment of the community radio sector. In Chile, a country not known for its progressive media policies, the central govern-ment has established a grant fund to support local and regional content production.[10] In Venezuela, often derided as a pariah state by Western governments and criticised by organizations promoting freedom of expression, community radio has now gained a strong foothold in the media system: according to AM-ARC International, community media has grown exponentially, from 60 stations in 2002, to 244 radio stations and 36 television stations in 2010.[11]

All these policies have the possibility of being corrupted and broadcasting licenses for community stations can be granted discretionally and be used to generate support for particular political parties or individuals. Nevertheless recognizing this model of content production readdresses a fundamental form of inequality: that of access to the airwaves. Latin American governments should however not only 'tolerate' community and non-profit media, but should actively encourage its development as a mechanism to reduce media concentration and to shrink the political influence of huge broadcasting corporations that have for too long been intimately associated with corrupt and anti-democratic regimes.

Notes

1. See Silvio Waisbord, "Latin America," in *Public Sentinel: News Media & Governance Reform*, ed. Pippa Norris (Washington, DC: World Bank, 2010), 305–28.

2. Eli Noam, "Mexico's Media Concentration and Ownership in Global Comparison," April 2014, accessed March 8, 2016, http://www.senado.gob.mx/comisiones/radio_tv_cine/docs/Eli_Noam.pdf.

3. Juan Enrique Huerta-Wong and Rodrigo Gómez García, "Concentración y Diversidad de los Medios de Comunicación y las Telecomunicaciones en México," *Comunicación y Sociedad* 19, (2013):113–52.

4. Foreign & Commonwealth Office, "Mexico: Challenging Telecoms Monopolies: Commercial Opportunities—March 2014," April 16, 2014, accessed March 9, 2016, https://www.gov.uk/government/publications/mexico-challenging-telecoms-monopolies-commercial-opportunities

-march-2014/mexico-challenging-telecoms-monopolies-commercial-opportunities-march-2014#contents.

5. Office of the Special Rapporteur for Freedom of Expression, *2010 Special Report on Freedom of Expression in Mexico,* March 4, 2011, accessed March 8, 2016, http://www.oas.org/en/iachr/expression/docs/reports/countries/2010%20FINAL%20CIDH%20Relator%C3%ADa%20Informe%20Mexico%20Libex_eng.pdf.

6. AMARC, *Situacion de las Radios Comunitarias en México*, July 2012, accessed March 9, 2016, http://www.amarcmexico.org/phocadownloadpap/informe_radios_com_2011_2012.pdf.

7. Article 19, "IFETEL Suspende Senal de dos Radio Comunitarias de Moreloso y Puebla," August 6, 2014, accessed March 8, 2016, http://www.period istasenlinea.org/07-08-2014/34317.

8. Rodrigo Gómez García, "Media Reform in Latin America: Communication Policies and Debate," *The Political Economy of Communication* 1, no. 1, (2013), accessed March 8, 2016, http://www.polecom.org/index.php/polecom/article/view/16/146.

9. Interpress Service, "Media Moguls Vow to Fight New Argentine Media Law," *Media Alliance*, October 12, 2009, accessed March 9, 2016, http://www.media-alliance.org/article.php?id=1801.

10. Gobierno de Chile, "Con aporte del Fondo de Medios de Comunicacion Publican Guia para Adultos Mayors en Punta Arenas," November 4, 2015, accessed March 9, 2016, http://fondodemedios.gob.cl/?p=8103.

11. AMARC, *Informe Annual: Diversidad y Pluralismo en la Radiodifusion*, 2010, accessed March 8, 2016, http://www.scribd.com/doc/253856058/Diversidad-y-Pluralismo-en-la-Radiodifusion-Informe-Anual-AMARC-2010.

21

The Best of Times and the Worst of Times: Dissent, Surveillance, and the Limits of the Liberal State

Natalie Fenton

For now, know that every border you cross, every purchase you make, every call you dial, every cellphone tower you pass, friend you keep, site you visit and subject line you type is in the hands of a system whose reach is unlimited, but whose safeguards are not.
—Edward Snowden to Laura Poitras, 2013 (Citizenfour)

The system that Snowden refers to is part of what has become known as mass surveillance activities by state authorities that stretch the very limits of what we might think of as liberal states.

A 2011 report by Freedom House on *Freedom on the Net* documents the increase in extent and diversity of Internet restrictions around the world. Daniel Calingaert[1] reports that these include 'bans on social media applications, denial of Internet access, intermediary liability for service providers, online surveillance, and digital attacks.' They also set out how both authoritarian and democratic governments engage willfully in a range of activities that include restricting and intimidating certain forms of online content; putting pressure on Internet service providers to monitor and remove certain types

of content and organizations deemed troublesome; employing 'just-in-time' blocking through distributed denial of service
(DDoS) attacks with the purpose of freezing oppositional organizations at vital political moments as well as targeted and
blanket surveillance.

This is commonly understood in authoritarian regimes
where the disabling of instant messaging services during periods of unrest, and the tracking, arresting, and torturing of
protestors who are active online, are well-known.[2] But post-
Snowden we now need to readily acknowledge that mass surveillance activities are equally at home in liberal states where
some of the most illiberal surveillance activities often exceed
the limits of our most liberal imaginations.

In 2013 Ed Snowden revealed a number of mass-surveil-
lance programmes undertaken by the National Security Agency
(NSA)—the phone and Internet interception specialist of the
United States—and the Government Communication Head-
quarters (GCHQ) in the United Kingdom. Snowden exposed
the extent to which private companies such as Google, Apple,
Microsoft, and Facebook are cooperating with intelligence
agencies[3] and collecting vast swathes of personal information
and metadata in a wholesale spying operation. Such actions are
claimed to be justifiable on the grounds of anti-terrorism and
the defeat of cybercrime, but it is easy to see just how such massive powers of unfreedom can be exploited for non-progressive
ends that undermine liberal democratic norms relating to individual rights and constitutionalism. The push towards the
securitization of cyberspace appears to be mainly defensive,
but Ronald Deibert and Rafal Rohozinski[4] also outline the pursuit of offensive capabilities enabling governments to wage

cyberattacks for political ends, a practice which they argue is increasingly commonplace.

Mass surveillance by governments on citizens contradicts basic democratic practice—it is super-Stasi on a grand scale enabled by big data capture. Mass surveillance is promiscuous by definition. A practice justified on the grounds of the pre-emption of terrorism. Pre-emption means everyone who disagrees with government policy is a potential threat and a potential target of surveillance programmes. Citizenfour, the documentary of the Snowden revelations, reported that there were an incredible 1.2 million Americans on the US government's watch list of people under surveillance as a potential threat or suspect.

Of course, our liberal democracies seek to establish the legitimacy of governments' monitoring capacity through legal frameworks. The Data Retention Directive in the European Union that became policy in 2006 required Internet service providers and telecommunications companies to store and make freely available to authorities details of all communications data—who, what, when, where—on all their users. The directive was implemented by the majority of European countries in 2009 then later overturned by the European Court of Human Rights in 2014. However, post-Snowden, many states have simply replaced the directive with national law and in the process have sought to increase the legality of data sweeping and storing.

In the United Kingdom, the Investigatory Powers Act 2016, known as the 'Snoopers' Charter', allows for almost every digital action to be logged, intercepted by intelligence agencies, and subject to scrutiny. The Act contains some of the most intrusive surveillance powers imaginable. It makes government hacking legal, bulk data sets can be collected and mined and encrypted services subject to state restrictions. It is legislation that has been criticized as using terrorist attacks as an excuse to override civil liberties, opening the door to indiscriminate and disproportionate surveillance. But this did nothing to impede its progress. There is nothing that is liberal about it.

In order for such practices to be possible, corporations must share their data supplies with government. Corporations benefit from government contracts. And so security software firms willingly weaken the security of their products or infect citizens' computers with malware which enables the authorities to see their screen or use their webcam, allowing governments to collect, store, and analyse simply astonishing amounts of data. For some Internet companies this causes problems for their brand image of communicative freedom and user autonomy but they too are complicit. Through their desire to better target advertising and monetise social media in particular, they increase and enhance the data available for state surveillance. In July 2014 Twitter acquired an image search company called Madbits to enable it to analyse its users through their photographs in order to improve the accuracy of their advertising placement. Once the data exists, restricting its usage to personal purposes has become virtually impossible, whether companies choose to share their data or are forced to.

And of course, every minute of every day ordinary citizens also willingly participate in mass surveillance through our online interactions, especially through social media and phone use. Every Internet search, every email, every text message, every phone call, every time you use your bank card; anywhere there is Wi-Fi or a router—in your home, in the coffee shop, in the workplace, in the classroom, at the cinema, in the gym—if you have access to a network your presence is being recorded.

One of the contradictions of the digital age is that just as it opens up all of our digital comings and goings to monitoring and monetising, so it is also argued to massively enhance our ability to forge alliances, respond rapidly to concerns or political events, organise protests, and mobilise dissent with minimal resources and bureaucracy, empowering individuals and strengthening civil society.[5] And as new communication technologies enable disparate protest groups to forge transnational alliances and affinities, the Internet may well have ushered in a new vibrant form of political activism, even though its consequences may not be the ones that were intended or that can necessarily deliver the democratic gains that were hoped for. Networks are not *inherently* liberatory: the Internet does not contain the essence of openness that will lead us directly to democracy.

Technologies are conceived and designed to work within the economic and political system of which they are a part. They are enmeshed within systems of power, as Andrew Feenberg[6] argues. Technology and capitalism have developed together. Similarly, the practices of digital media *may* be liberating for the user, but not necessarily democratising for society. Any argument for the liberating role of new technologies and enhancement of radical politics needs then also to be assessed in the wider context of the increasing securitization of cyberspace that has severe implications for basic freedoms.[7]

If you protest against austerity measures and disagree with neoliberal policies, the Internet and particularly social media at once enable the mobilization of protest on an unprecedented scale and also subject protest practices to easy and increased surveillance. Internet surveillance programmes such as Prism and Tempora target all social media use and enable particular groups and people to be scrutinized with the aim of suppressing protest activity.[8] The consequences of such programmes for legitimate political activism are profound.

Suppressing protest involves predictive policing, which relies upon social media data to provide police with information that will feed into their attempts to limit the size, length, and impact of protests. They do this through intercepting communications infrastructures, predicting the movement of a protest so they can 'kettle' people in contained spaces and direct and dispel legitimate protest activity.[9] Such practices exist alongside an enormous increase in others also designed to preempt dissent, including anti-union legislation, criminalization of protest, and in some cases, incarceration, making it ever more difficult to launch protests and carry out demonstrations within the law at a national level.

If freedom of assembly and protest are one of the basic tenets of liberalism, it is hard to conclude anything other than that in neoliberal times, we have reached the very end of its limits.

Notes

1. Daniel Calingaert, "Challenges for International Policy," in *Liberation Technology: Social Media and the Struggle for Democracy*, eds. Larry Diamond and Marc F. Plattner (Baltimore, MD: John Hopkins University Press, 2012), 157–74.
2. Evgeny Morozov, "Whither Internet Control?," in *Liberation Technology: Social Media and the Struggle for Democracy*, eds. Larry Diamond and Marc F. Plattner (Baltimore, MD: John Hopkins University Press, 2012), 47–62; Rebecca Mackinnon, "China's 'Networked Authoritarianism'" in *Liberation Technology: Social Media and the Struggle for Democracy*, eds. Larry Diamond and Marc F. Plattner (Baltimore, MD: John Hopkins University Press, 2012),

78–94; Ronald Deibert, "International Mechanisms of Cyberspace Control," in *Liberation Technology: Social Media and the Struggle for Democracy*, eds. Larry Diamond and Marc F. Plattner (Baltimore, MD: John Hopkins University Press, 2012), 33–46.

3. Ronald Deibert, "International Mechanisms of Cyberspace Control."

4. Ronald Deibert and Rafal Rohozinski, "Liberation vs. Control: The Future of Cyberspace," in *Liberation Technology: Social Media and the Struggle for Democracy*, eds. Larry Diamond and Marc F. Plattner (Baltimore, MD: John Hopkins University Press, 2012), 18–32.

5. Natalie Fenton, *Digital, Political, Radical* (London: Polity, 2016).

6. Andrew Feenberg, "Subversive Rationalisation: Technology, Power and Democracy," in *Technology and the Politics of Knowledge*, eds. Andrew Feenberg and Alastair Hannay (Bloomington: Indiana University Press, 1995); Andrew Feenberg, *Transforming Technology: A Critical Theory Revisited*, (Oxford: Oxford University Press, 2001).

7. Evgeny Morozov, "Whither Internet Control?".

8. Lina Dencik and Oliver Leistert eds., *Critical Perspectives on Social Media Protest: Between Control and Emancipation*. (London: Rowman and Littlefield, 2015).

9. Greg Elmer, "Pre-empting Dissent: From Participatory Policing to Collaborative Filmmaking," in *Critical Perspectives on Social Media Protest: Between Control and Emancipation*, eds. Lina Dencik and Oliver Leistert (London: Rowman and Littlefield, 2015).

Liberalism and Education

Higher education is premised on liberal values of tolerance, enlightenment, reason, and intellectual development; it has been organised, however, on less than liberal values of social stratification, exclusion, patronage, and capitalist development. The idea of the public university has long been countered by the reality of a cloistered one and a commitment to equality undermined by a capitulation to elites.

In current circumstances, the concept of a liberal university education faces even more robust challenges as an untrammelled economic liberalism attempts to redesign the architecture of higher education across the world. Higher tuition fees, increased managerialism, an emphasis on employability for the majority of students, a fetishisation of metrics and impact in relation to research, and the general implantation of market values into higher education—this is the reality for universities well beyond just the United Kingdom and United States.

In this context, should we mourn the passing of the liberal notion of higher education and how should we respond to the new demands of neoliberal restructuring of the institutions and practices that make up the academy? Should we attempt to protect liberal values in the face of a neoliberal backlash? Is there a future (or even a present) for liberal arts beyond elite campuses? This section reflects on these and many other questions that confront the assault on the very idea of a public higher education.

22

Patrimonial Capitalism Re-Booted and the End of the Liberal University

John Holmwood

The university was once central to the liberal imagination as the repository of reason and culture (as argued in Germany by Kant and Humboldt, for example), or as a community of scholars and students engaged in the education of character and intellect (as argued by Newman in Britain). Of course, these ideals were tied to an upper-class status order from which women, religious minorities, and the broad mass of the population were excluded, including by formal segregation on the grounds of race as in the United States. In England, this embodiment of status extended to the physical character of the old collegiate Universities of Oxford and Cambridge, and was mirrored in the public schools of Eton, Harrow, Westminster, and Winchester, with their quadrangles, chapels, and dining halls.

The high-minded view of the university, however, was not an accurate description even in the nineteenth century, when perceived requirements of industrial development contributed to a shift in focus away from the liberal professions towards the needs of business. In this context, new ideas of the university—of civic universities oriented to local needs—began to predominate, especially in the United States with land grant universities offering a robust and practical alternative to the ivy-clad private colleges.

For Max Weber,[1] this reflected a new 'democratic ethos', one that he thought would give rise to bureaucratisation and a capitalist-like division of labour, which would in turn undermine a scholarly vocation dependent on freedom from the requirement to earn a living. However, the impact of that ethos is perhaps not best represented in the era in which he lamented it, but by the much later development of the public university in the post–World War II period. Alongside the older functions of the university—the reproduction of culture and its contribution to industrial development—a new function of serving mass democratic participation was added. Here the university would be asked to serve social mobility and also to contribute to the effective practice of democratic citizenship.

This can be understood, in part, as an extension of liberal rights—of expression, free choice of occupation, and equality before the law—into the social realm. On the one hand, a divided status order was to be dissolved into a single order of citizenship, in which education was perceived as a social right.[2] On the other hand, social rights (to health, education, etc.,) were also perceived as necessary to ameliorate market-based class inequalities.

This was the moment of the public university, perhaps best exemplified by the California Master Plan of Clark Kerr[3] and the reforms associated with the Robbins Report in the United Kingdom.[4] It was marked by a commitment to the expansion of participation in higher education as well as by the principle that such expansion should be through direct public funding. This reflected an increased consciousness of the wider public benefits of higher education—what Milton Friedman referred to as its 'neighbourhood effects'[5] beyond the private benefit understood in human capital terms. For Robbins and Kerr, alike, the secular decline of inequality meant that economic growth was inclusive and, thus, public funding of higher education available to all who could benefit (as Robbins put it) was justified, notwithstanding that unlike compulsory secondary education there could not be full participation and, therefore, there would also be a private benefit.

One paradox of publicly-funded education, first articulated by Weber and developed by Kerr, was that its democratic ethos would favour a practical orientation, both in terms of research and teaching, undermining the subjects that were at the core of the older status-oriented idea of the university. However, it would also give rise to the idea that the function of university education was not simply to provide a framework for a stable and democratic society, but to facilitate critical engagement with that society and its inequalities of power and condition.

Thomas Piketty[6] suggests that the period of 'social liberalism', of the articulation of social rights of citizenship to ameliorate inequalities of class and status, came to an end in Western countries in the early 1980s when the peculiar conditions that sustained it began to fade. Capitalism's logic is to widen inequality and, with the re-establishment of inequalities in wealth alongside inequalities in income, according to Piketty inheritance returns as an important principle in the reproduction of inequality.

It is in this context that the idea of the university is once again undergoing transformation in the light of neoliberal public policy and the privatisation of public services. Increasingly, education is perceived as an object of private capital investment, both through outsourcing of functions to for-profit companies and the direct entry of for-profit providers. At the same time, the private benefits of higher education to its graduate beneficiaries are used to justify the removal of public funding and the charging of fees. University managers collude in this process by using those benefits as the justification for the idea that fees should be ever higher.

As many have observed,[7] the neoliberal deregulation of labour markets has, at the same time, created a polarisation between good jobs and bad jobs, with the former too few to provide for all graduates, and graduate qualifications for many providing merely a bad job rather than no job. In this context, the pressure is to differentiate fees and courses, and, together with the status associations of supposed elite institutions, to create education as a positional good.

Universities no longer function to ameliorate social status and inequality, but are part of the new status order of a renewed patrimonial capitalism. What is significant, however, is that there is no university figure—no Kerr or Robbins—to step forward to articulate the idea of the university for the twenty-first century. A narrow utilitarianism prevails and vice chancellors are now brand managers, not stewards of culture and knowledge. Their universities are knowledge corporations, competing in a global market for higher education with their salary packages no different to those of other top executives and growing apace.

The neighbourhood effects of higher education are reserved for wealthy neighbourhoods and a grim regime of fitness training for a global race is reserved for the rest. The liberal idea of the university is gone. In the words of the UK government, that idea has lost its usefulness: 'It is for institutions themselves to decide their own structures. Some have found ingenious ways to combine profit-making and non profit-making arms. … A positive strategic commitment to remain at a certain size is one thing. A reluctant ossification and decline, caused by an inability to see how to change a structure that is thought to have outlived its usefulness, would be quite another.'[8]

But something more than the idea of the university is at stake. What is also at stake is the meaning of democracy and its possibility in circumstances of patrimonial capitalism and ever-widening inequalities.

Notes

1. Max Weber, "Science as a Vocation," in *From Max Weber: Essays in Sociology*, trans. & eds. Hans Heinrich Gerth and Charles Wright Mills (London: Routledge and Kegan Paul, 1947), 129–56.

2. Thomas H. Marshall, "Citizenship and Social Class: The Problem Stated," in *Citizenship and Social Class: And Other Essays* (Cambridge: Cambridge University Press, 1950), 1–85.

3. Clark Kerr, *The Uses of the University* (Cambridge, MA: Harvard University Press, 2001).

4. Robbins Report, *Higher Education: Report of the Committee Appointed by the Prime Minister under the Chairmanship of Lord Robbins 1961–63*. Cmnd 2154 (London: HMSO, 1963).

5. Milton Friedman, *Capitalism and Freedom* (Chicago: University of Chicago Press, 1962).

6. Thomas Piketty, *Capital in the Twenty-First Century* (Cambridge, MA: The Belknap Press of Harvard University Press, 2014).

7. Philip Brown, Hugh Lauder and David Ashton, *The Global Auction: The Broken Promises of Education, Jobs and Incomes* (Oxford: Oxford University Press, 2011); Arne Kalleberg, *Good Jobs, Bad Jobs: The Rise of Polarized and Precarious Employment Systems in the United States, 1970s to 2000s* (New York: Russell Sage Foundation, 2011).

8. Department for Business, Innovation and Science, *International Education: Global Growth and Prosperity*, July 2013, accessed March 1, 2016, https://www .gov.uk/government/uploads/system/uploads/attachment_data/file/340600/ bis-13-1081-international-education-global-growth-and-prosperity-revised.pdf.

23

When Liberals Fail to Defend Academic Freedom

Priyamvada Gopal

When North American universities reopened for the 2014–15 academic year, one name was missing controversially from the roster of fall courses at the University of Illinois, Urbana-Champaign (UIUC). Steven Salaita, an associate professor at Virginia Tech with a stellar research and teaching record, had a signed contract of appointment to a tenured post in UIUC's department of American Indian Studies. A few weeks before, the university suddenly dismissed Salaita who was awaiting the routine formality of a board of trustees endorsement.[1] He had resigned from his previous job. No official reason for the 'dehiring', to use its own parlance, was given by the university for several days until a vague statement from Chancellor Phyllis Wise referenced 'personal and disrespectful words or actions'.[2] This confirmed suspicions that the decision—taken without any academic consultation—had indeed been based on impassioned tweets that Salaita, a Palestinian-American, had posted during the first half of July as terrible destruction was wrought by the Israeli invasion of Gaza.

Significantly, only days before taking this action, the university had explicitly defended the right of its employees to voice controversial views as vehement pro-Israel campaigners had begun to petition it against Salaita's appointment, terming him, using familiar practice, an anti-Semite. The manufactured controversy, fuelled by the political predilections of influential donors, hinges upon a very small selection of tweets that Salaita had posted. They expressed anger at the massacres in Gaza and addressed the wearisome charge that criticism of the Israeli state equals anti-Semitism, a charge familiar to anyone who has dared venture disquiet with Israeli state policies and practices.

One tweet (protected speech in the United States) that was singled out as evidence of anti-Semitism was from July 19, 2014: 'Zionists: transforming "anti-Semitism" from something horrible into something honorable since 1948.' As several commentators have since pointed out, the tweet in itself—and certainly in the context of Salaita's other tweets, many of which explicitly condemn anti-Semitism—does the opposite of condoning anti-Semitism.[3] Within Twitter's 140 character limit, it notes that Zionists who reduce all criticism of even the worst actions of the state of Israel into anti-Semitism also traduce honourable opposition. Such routine misuse of a serious charge runs the grave danger of diminishing the gravity and reality of the phenomenon of anti-Semitism itself, doing its actual victims a real disservice.

As Michael Rothberg, chair of the English Department and himself a Holocaust scholar 'sensitive to expressions of anti-Semitism', notes in his excellent letter of dissent to Wise, Salaita's tweets were manifestly 'not expressions of antisemitism but criticism of how charges of antisemitism are used to excuse otherwise inexcusable actions'. He notes too that while a 'civil tone' may generally be preferable, certain occasions call for strong language (Salaita uses the F-word in one tweet) and an expansion of the idea of 'what constitutes an acceptable tone so that it is commensurate with the events at stake.'[4]

Even as hundreds of academics in North America and beyond, including many who teach at Urbana-Champaign, signed letters of protest and pledged not to undertake any professional services at the university, including refereeing and speaking engagements, one of the most striking aspects of the affair was the willingness of self-defined liberals to either mitigate or endorse the firing of Salaita. As such, the case has also thrown light on the limits of liberalism and its acquiescence to the encroaching depredations of the corporate managerial culture that now afflicts universities across the world. Apart from anything else, this is a case of high-handed administrative behaviour, increasing corporate influence (the board of trustees is composed of powerful business people who know little about scholarship or teaching), and the steady erosion of the vital principle of scholarly autonomy.

Before Wise—and then the trustees—put out statements defending their patently political and partisan decision—the chief attack dog for the anti-Salaita camp was prominent left-wing liberal academic, Professor Emeritus Cary Nelson, a former president of the American Association of University Professors (whose office-bearers have been swift to decry the decision and to distance themselves from him) and still a member, ironically, of its important Academic Freedom and Tenure Committee.

Praising Chancellor Wise for 'doing what had to be done', Nelson denounced Salaita's tweets with McCarthyite relish as 'venomous', 'loathsome', 'foul-mouthed … hate speech' and 'obsessively driven' on the matter of Israel–Palestine (hardly surprising in context given that the area constitutes one of Salaita's scholarly specialisms).[5]

Nelson was among the first to articulate the peculiar notion, now given as an official rationale for Salaita's dismissal, that students had a right to be protected from discomfort (slyly conflated with abuse) in the classroom and that strong views held outside the classroom posed a danger inside it. Academic freedom, Nelson opined, 'does not require you to hire someone whose views you consider despicable' (though it remains unclear who the 'you' is, given that Salaita had earned scholarly approval after a rigorous search process).[6] On social media, liberals agreed that while they didn't precisely defend the university's decision, Salaita had, unfortunately for him, 'tested the limits of free speech' and found them—though it remains unclear who determines these limits. While academic freedom had 'of course' to be defended, Salaita was 'the wrong case' for such defence, having 'crossed' some patently imaginary 'line' to do with 'civility' and 'collegiality'.

The latter two are, of course, buzzwords of determinate vagueness intended precisely to keep up, as Wise does in her statement, the banal pretence of defending 'diversity' and 'dialogue' while wielding a wild card intended to swiftly mark their limits as decided from on high. Speak truth to power but power will decide when enough truth has been spoken. Indeed, Wise's statement itself is an exemplary exercise in managed diversity with its exhaustive encomiums, on the one hand, to principles of academic freedom, diversity, contentious discourse, robust debate, critical arguments, difficult discussions, differing perspectives, confronted viewpoints, and challenged assumptions, and on the other, a litany of vague and confused disciplinary notions whose content and provenance will also be decided from on high. They include 'respect for students' rights as individuals', a 'civil and productive manner', no 'demeaning and abusing viewpoints', 'valuing students as human beings', and dialogue that is 'civil and thoughtful' and 'mutually respectful'—all of which seems unexceptional enough but can hardly be specified objectively, particularly in relation to difficult emotive issues. The UIUC Trustees backed Wise's statement, duly deeming it as 'thoughtful' in its affirmation of campuses as 'safe harbors' for making 'productive citizens' and 'valu[ing] civility as much as scholarship'.[7]

In November 2015, Steven Salaita and UIUC came to a financial settlement. As Salaita noted subsequently, the term 'settlement' remains 'largely meaningless if the conditions that produced [his] firing remain intact, at UIUC and elsewhere'.[8] Those conditions not only remain intact but are in danger of intensifying with increased corporate and managerial control of research and teaching. The deliberate and vile conflation of campaigning critiques of Israeli policy with anti-Semitism has been given official sanction in the United Kingdom with recent guidelines that prevent boycott of Israeli goods connected to settlement territories by governmental and publicly funded bodies.[9] British academics, who do not have the protection of tenure, are even more vulnerable to charges of infringing vague notions of 'collegiality' and 'civility', generally used to police politically 'difficult' colleagues. Used disproportionately as a disciplinary mechanism against 'mouthy' women and ethnic minorities the 'civil' in 'civility' is also generally the 'civil in 'civilise'. Opposing and undoing these repressive regimes with justice within and beyond the university remains the task in front of us.

Notes

1. Jodi S. Cohen, "U. of I. Pulls Professor's Job Offer after Tweets Criticizing Israel," *Chicago Tribune*, August 14, 2014, accessed March 1, 2016, http://www .chicagotribune.com/news/nationworld/chi-illinois-professor-israel -20140813-story.html.

2. John K. Wilson, "Chancellor Phyllis Wise Explains the Firing of Steven Salaita," *Academe Blog* (blog), August 22, 2014, accessed March 1, 2016, https://academeblog.org/2014/08/22/chancellor-phyllis-wise-explains-the -firing-of-steven-salaita.

3. Corey Robin, "What Exactly Did Steven Salaita Mean by That Tweet?," August 8, 2014, accessed March 2, 2016, http://coreyrobin.com/2014/08/08/ what-exactly-did-steven-salaita-mean-by-that-tweet.

4. Robert Mackey, "Professor's Angry Tweets on Gaza Cost Him a Job," *New York Times*, September 12, 2014, http://www.nytimes.com/2014/09/13/world/ middleeast/professors-angry-tweets-on-gaza-cost-him-a-job.html?_r=0.

5. Scott Jaschik, "Out of a Job," *Inside Higher Ed*, August 6, 2014, https://www .insidehighered.com/news/2014/08/06/u-illinois-apparently-revokes-job -offer-controversial-scholar.

6. Peter Schmidt, "Denial of Job to Harsh Critic of Israel Divides Advocates of Academic Freedom," *Chronicle of Higher Education*, August 7, 2014, accessed March 1, 2016, http://chronicle.com/article/Denial-of-Job-to-Harsh-Critic/ 148211.

7. Christopher G. Kennedy et al., "An Atmosphere for Learning," mass email message, August 22, 2014, accessed March 2, 2016, https://cfaillinois.files .wordpress.com/2014/08/civility-massmail.pdf.

8. Steven Salaita, "I Will Always Condemn Injustice No Matter the State of My Employment,' *The Nation*, November 13, 2015, accessed March 1, 2016, http:// www.thenation.com/article/steven-salaita-i-will-always-condemn-injustice -no-matter-the-state-of-my-employment.

9. Rowena Mason, "Councils and NHS Trusts to Be Blocked from Boycotting Israeli Products," *Guardian*, February 15, 2016, accessed March 1, 2016, http:// www.theguardian.com/society/2016/feb/15/councils-and-nhs-trusts-to-be -blocked-from-boycotting-israeli-products.

24

Apprentice or Student? The New Old Choice for Young People

Patrick Ainley

Among the many promises made in the 2015 UK General Election was this from David Cameron: 'We will create three million more apprenticeships. ... That's three million more engineers, accountants, project managers.'[1] The non sequitur is blatantly delusional if Cameron believes it or it is misleadingly dishonest if he does not. Yet it is no more illusory than the promises made to university students that degrees guarantee the secure, professional jobs to which most aspire.

The two false promises are connected by Matthew Hancock, former-minister in the Department for Business Innovation and Skills, declaring in 2014 that, in order to 'rebalance' school-leaver destinations, 'alongside universities, apprenticeships will be the new norm'[2] for people eighteen years of age and older. With the raising of the participation age (in school, FE, or training) to eighteen in 2015, Hancock's 'new norm' presented all school-leavers with just two options—apprentice or student.

In fact, large numbers of boys follow neither of these two official routes, but leave school for unregulated employment. No one knows where since the Careers Service has been privatized out of existence. A minor moral panic followed over these 'lost boys' who do not show up in further or higher education (where women are now 60 per cent of undergraduates), or on apprenticeships where the majority are also female. So now widening participation to working-class boys is to be added to the key indicators that will allow HE institutions to charge higher fees under the proposed Teaching Excellence Framework.[3]

The 'lost boys' were also supposed to be mopped up by the expansion of apprenticeships funded by the levy on large employers that the Chancellor, George Osborne, unexpectedly announced in his 2015 autumn spending review. This, however, only provoked bitter recriminations from the employers' Confederation of British Industry because, as Martin Allen's on-going research shows,[4] most employers do not want or need apprenticeships, let alone to have to pay for them. The few who do, already pay for them themselves.

Allen's work also shows most apprenticeships continue to be low-skilled and dead-end. Of the approximately two million that have been created since 2010, the majority have been filled by adults, with many examples of existing staff being reclassified as 'apprentices' to allow employers to access government subsidies. Two-thirds of apprenticeships are only equivalent to GCSE, a level to which most young people are already qualified. They generally last only a year or less and in most cases provide no employment guarantees and no opportunities to progress to a higher level, though they are supposed to do both. They are therefore not really apprenticeships at all but 'Another Great Training Robbery',[5] as officially confirmed by a damning Ofsted report at the end of 2015.[6]

Unlike post-war apprenticeships associated with manufacturing, the employment areas where today's apprenticeships are most easily available are in stereotypically feminine routine office work, low-skill retail, or health and social care. There have been some changes so that by 2014 at least two-thirds of starts were by people under twenty-four, though only a quarter of these (120,000) were under nineteen. More young people also started Advanced level schemes, even if numbers are low—just 35,000 starts in 2013–2014—while the 9,000 Higher level apprenticeships starts in 2015, which include some higher education, are not likely to create an 'alternative route into work' as the government claims.[7]

Until now, the training of apprentices was carried out by private providers, which then claimed government funding but the new levy of 0.5 per cent of the wages bill of large employers (approximately 2 per cent of all employers) will raise nearly £3 billion. Although potentially doubling apprenticeship funding, it cannot be regarded as a panacea, the main reason being the deregulated, low-skill labour market within which apprenticeships operate. Most apprentice training is therefore restricted to narrow workplace-based National Vocational Qualifications with functional skills included for those without A-C GCSE maths and English. FE colleges would be the obvious place to deliver additional education alongside work-based training but they are being merged and closed under on-going area reviews.

Instead, FE students are being decanted into mass HE as nearly all universities desperately compete to cram in students paying more for less on whom their funding now depends. This makes it easier than ever to get into university as they poach students from one another, creaming off applicants who thought they were heading for more middling institutions but who can now trade up the hierarchy—trade down from the universities' point of view. As a result, in 2015, notwithstanding some pick up in the economy, relentless propaganda for apprenticeships and a demographic fall in numbers of eighteen-to-nineteen-year-olds, more applied in the absence of any other alternative.

Young people thus rejected apprenticeships in favour of debt for overpriced and often insubstantial degrees, knowing that—as long as they could avoid a 'deadly Desmond' (2.2) and graduate with a 1st or 2.1, which over 70 per cent now do—they would be better off than with an apprenticeship. Especially as employers usually prefer graduates to apprentices for increasingly routinized work and a good degree at least gets your foot in the door for selection to semi-professional, graduatised employment.

Nevertheless, there is a cross-party and educationalist consensus on the need for apprenticeships as part of a vocational route for other people's children 'who are not academic but want to do something practical', as it is often patronizingly put. Apprenticeships sound simultaneously modern and reassuringly traditional so that many parents, teachers, and school-leavers want to believe in them, as they do also in the power of education. They also have the appeal to policy makers and pundits of magically turning the deregulated UK service-led economy into a productive German one—as in David Cameron's wishful thinking above.

Yet since 2008, numbers in low-paid, insecure, and often part-time jobs have ratcheted up to include perhaps half of new entrants to employment. This fuels public hysteria about academic exams that function as proxies for more or less expensively acquired cultural capital as students desperately run up a down-escalator of inflating qualifications to avoid falling into the structural insecurity beneath. For, however employable schools, colleges, and universities claim to make their students, education cannot guarantee employment. The perception of this problem needs to change: from seeing young people as having to be prepared for employment by earlier and earlier specialization for vocations that may not exist by the time they complete their training. Instead, the starting point should be a common general but not academic foundational schooling to eighteen giving entitlement to progression for citizens fit for a variety of labours.

This implies confronting the possibilities of flexibility but avoiding the current situation where there are more people in the workforce but many are paid little for unregulated employment so that many people eighteen years of age and older are overqualified for, and underemployed in, the jobs on offer. An alternative economic framework is required but not necessarily the right to work with which the orthodox Left continues to operate in a post-war collectivised model of the labour market. Instead, we should encourage students and young people to learn about work and not just to learn *to* work.

Notes

1. David Cameron, "A Britain That Gives Every Child the Best Start in Life," speech on February 2, 2015, accessed 1 March 2016, http://press .conservatives.com/post/109906886845/david-cameron-a-britain-that -gives-every-child.

2. Matthew Hancock, speech to Association of Education Learning Providers, June 2, 2014, accessed 1 March 2016, https://www.gov.uk/government/news/ minister-reinforces-importance-of-apprenticeship-reforms.

3. Department for Business, Innovation & Skills, *Fulfilling Our Potential: Teaching Excellence, Social Mobility and Student Choice*, green paper (London: HMSO, 2015).

4. Martin Allen, "Mr Cameron's Three Million Apprenticeships," *Forum* 57 no. 3, (2015): 355–60. doi:10.15730/forum.2015.57.3.355.

5. Martin Allen, "Another Great Training Robbery or a Real Alternative for Young People?: Apprenticeships at the Start of the 21st Century," *Radicaledbks* (blog), January 2016, accessed 1 March 2016, https://radicaledbks.files .wordpress.com/2013/09/another-great-training-robbery4.pdf.

6. Ofsted, *Apprenticeships: Developing Skills for Future Prosperity,* October 22, 2015, accessed 1 March 2016, https://www.gov.uk/government/publications/ apprenticeships-developing-skills-for-future-prosperity.

7. Skills Funding Agency, *Higher and Degree Apprenticeships* (London: HMSO, 2015), accessed 7 March 2016, https://www.gov.uk/government/uploads/ system/uploads/attachment_data/file/412019/Higher_Apprenticeship_and_ Degree_Apprenticeship_Delivery_from_April_2015_to_April_2016.pdf.

25

New Managerialism in Education: The Organisational Form of Neoliberalism

Kathleen Lynch

With the rise of neoliberalism as a system of values,[1] there is an increasing attempt to offload the cost of education, health care, and public services generally on to the individual. Allied to this, there is a growing movement to privatise those areas of public services that could be run for-profit, including higher education.

New managerialism represents the organisational arm of neoliberalism. It is the mode of governance designed to realise the neoliberal project through the institutionalising of market principles in the governance of organisations. In the public sector (and increasingly in civil society bodies) it involves the prioritisation of private (for-profit) sector values of efficiency and productivity in the regulation of public bodies, on the assumption that the former is superior to the latter.[2]

While it would be a mistake to view new managerialism as a unitary whole, implemented consistently across differing cultural and economic contexts, nevertheless in the redesign of public service provision, key features of managerialism include: an emphasis on outputs over inputs; the close monitoring of employee performance and the encouragement of self-monitoring through the widespread use of performance indicators, rankings, league tables, and performance management. The decentralisation of budgetary and personal authority to line managers, combined with the retention of power and control at central level, and the introduction of new and more casualised contractual employment arrangements, are also key features that serve to reduce costs and exercise control.

New managerialism is further characterised by significant changes in nomenclature. There is a declining use of language that frames public services in terms of citizens' rights, public welfare, and solidarity and a growing emphasis on language that defines the citizen's relationship to the state in terms of market values, be it that of customers, service users, and competitors. There is a deliberate attempt to elide the differences between public and private interests. New configurations of public–private relationships are designated as 'partnerships' erasing the differences between public and private interest values, between providing a service at cost and only providing a service if it is profitable.

As it involves the inculcation of market values and practices into the regulation and organisation of public services in particular (and increasingly voluntary and community organizations), new managerialism focuses service providers on outputs measured in terms of performance indicators and rankings (often regardless of inputs or resources). It is operationalised through the language of choice, competition, and service users; it promotes the decentralisation of budgetary and personal authority to line managers, and project-led contractual employment arrangements rather than permanency. And it endorses strong market-type accountability in public sector spending. The net effect is that meeting financial and other targets is a priority, and success in meeting targets is measured through public audits. The development of quasi-markets for services is also a key goal, and rankings feed directly into this process; internal markets operate as a further form of control through competition and public surveillance of public sector services.

New managerialism is not a neutral management strategy therefore; it is a political project, borne out of a radical change in the organisation of capitalism. As such, it is embedded in a complex series of social, political, and economic organizational changes that are tied to neoliberalism in particular. It rests on the assumption that the market is the primary producer of cultural logic and value and that universities and higher education (and public services) generally are best run through the deployment of market logic and market mechanisms. It reduces first-order social and moral values to second-order principles: trust, integrity, care, and solidarity with others are subordinated to regulation, control, and competition. In this regard it provides a unique type of moral guidance for businesses and organizations modelled on businesses, including hospitals, schools, welfare offices, and housing departments.

When managerialist practices achieve hegemonic control within public service organizations, they parasitise and weaken those very values on which the organization depends.

While few would question the value of efficiency, in terms of maximizing the use of available resources, the difficulty with managerialism is that it does not just prioritise efficiency, it suppresses other organizational values so that they become incidental to the running of public bodies. The net effect of the devaluation of moral purposes is that public services, such as education and health care, are increasingly defined as commodities to be delivered on the market to customers who can afford to buy them. They are no longer defined as capacity-building public goods. Rights to health care, housing, and education are delegitimised within this framework and what were once human rights are transformed into commodities bought at market value. Within this frame, it is inevitable that only those who can purchase goods such as health care, quality elder care, child care, and higher education will have access to it over time.

As new managerialism reduces economic, educational and social problems, and moral dilemmas, to issues of governance and regulation, ethical considerations are construed as management issues that new managerial regimes can resolve. The political and social purposes of education, for example, are treated as secondary considerations. Commercial values are institutionalized in systems and processes: schools and colleges change from being centres of learning to *service-delivery operations* with productivity targets.

While the nurturing of learners has an outcome dimension in education, for example, the care-related gains from education are generally not measurable in the short term within a metric. The inevitable, if unintended, correlate of evaluating merit through measurement is that the core principle of caring in health, education, and other public services is subordinated to output. Even if the caring dimensions of welfare and public services could be monitored and measured through matrices, the very doing of this would force people into the calculation of other-centredness that would undermine the very principle of relatedness and mutuality that is at the heart of teaching and learning, welfare and health care.

Given its alignment with neoliberal values, managerialism also implicitly endorses a concept of the citizen that is market-led. All forms of education, for example, but especially higher education, are defined in terms of human capital acquisition. The purpose of education is increasingly limited to developing the neoliberal citizen, the competitive economic actor and cosmopolitan worker built around a calculating, entrepreneurial, and detached self. A narcissistic actuarialism[3] is encouraged and new educational subjectivities are created. Education itself becomes a way of managing market risks in a highly deregulated world. The concept of working in or for the public service (or the community and voluntary sectors) is diminished.

Notes

1. David Harvey, *A Brief History of Neoliberalism* (Oxford: Oxford University Press, 2005).
2. Kathleen Lynch, Bernie Grummell and Dympna Devine, *New Managerialism in Education: Commercialisation, Carelessness and Gender* (Basingstoke, UK: Palgrave Macmillan, 2012).
3. Michael A. Peters, "The New Prudentialism in Education: Actuarial Rationality and the Entrepreneurial Self," *Educational Theory* 55, no. 2 (2005): 123–37. doi:10.1111/j.0013-2004.2005.00002.x.

26

The Liberal Arts in Neoliberal Times[1]

Toby Miller

The United States sometimes seems unremittingly utilitarian on the one hand (business), and sedulously superstitious on the other (religion). But it is far more than those economic and religious designations might suggest.

Just as medievalism was invented and remains curated in the Midwest, and just as so-so writers can be confident that their papers will be purchased by college libraries there, so there is a disinterested, deeply scholarly side to US life. It is reflected in the little liberal arts colleges that dot the country, where tweedy 'profs' with sensible shoes (as they are lovingly called) rub shoulders with 'lesbians-until-graduation' (as they are misogynistically labeled) in leafy surroundings.

But the last thirty years have changed things. The neoliberal epoch has ushered in a dramatic transformation.

The humanities' share of majors stands at 8 to 12 per cent of the nation's 110,000 undergraduates, depending on which count you favor in a massive system that has decentralized record keeping. That's less than half the figure from the 1960s, and the lowest point since World War II.

Between 1970–71 and 2003–04, English majors declined from 7.6 to 3.9 per cent of the national total, other languages and literatures from 2.5 to 1.3 per cent, philosophy and religious studies from 0.9 to 0.7 per cent, and history from 18.5 to 10.7 per cent. By contrast, business enrolments increased 176 per cent, and communication studies shot up 616 per cent. Many of the wee liberal arts colleges have shuttered their doors. Almost half the remaining ones see students majoring in business.

Downturns in student interest align with two phenomena: prolonged recessions, such as those curated by Republican administrations from Ronald Reagan to both George Bush Sr. and Jr.; and an emerging passion for seemingly instrumental study areas such as business and government, especially in public schools designed for the proletariat and the middle class. These massive second-tier state schools are the physical heart of US higher education, where the vast majority of students are enrolled. And areas such as literature and history are not vastly popular there. Hardly a surprise when student debt stands at one trillion dollars.[2]

Fancy schools for children of the *bourgeoisie* and their favored subaltern representatives, notably the Ivy Leagues, continue to encourage young people who are finding themselves en route to the elite to do so via the doubting Dane and the suiciding Plath. The rest of the country doesn't think it can afford the privilege.

The numbers are not just about enrolment trends in abstraction. They reflect students' neoliberal investment in human capital, as per Gary Becker[3] and his chorines. And they are to do with the universities' own values and Federal Government policies.

Compared with other fields, tenure-track hiring in language and literature occurs at two-thirds the national average. In 2009, just 53 per cent of humanities faculty was in full-time employment, and an even smaller proportion in tenure-track positions. A similar discount applies to salaries. In 2003, health academics were paid an average of $6,000 more than in 1987, during which time the humanities average declined by $1,000; in 2005–06, a business academic cost twice as much as a humanities one, compared to one and a half times as much twenty years earlier.

And research support? National Science Foundation (NSF) grants went from being five times the size of their National Endowment for the Humanities (NEH) equivalents in 1979 to thirty-three times in 1997. In 2007, the NEH received 0.5 per cent of the National Institutes of Health's budget and 3 per cent of the NSF's, while in 2010 a pitiful 0.45 per cent of Federal research support went to the humanities.

The 2009 American Recovery and Reinvestment Act,[4] the Keynesian salvation from the global financial crisis, saw the NSF receive three billion dollars. The Act provided not a cent to humanities research. Barack Obama's 2011 State of the Union address[5] called for increased expenditure on research, education, and teachers of mathematics and science. He did not mention the humanities.

The story is gloomy and dismal.

But that is a story about the traditional humanities, the ones we think of when we read the *New York Times* gleefully making fun of literary theory or queer readings at its annual denunciation[6] of the Modern Language Association's conference.

And the fact is that there are two humanities in the United States. The distinction between them, which is far from absolute, but heuristically and statistically persuasive, places literature, history, and philosophy on one side (Humanities One) and communication studies on the other (Humanities Two).

Humanities One primarily resides in Research One private universities, liberal arts colleges, and a few privileged state schools. Humanities One is venerable, powerful, and tends to determine how the sector is discussed in public—but almost no one studies it.

Humanities Two is the humanities of everyday state schools and is focused more on undergraduates' job prospects—but has no media profile. Humanities One dominates rhetorically. Humanities Two dominates numerically. Thousands of grad students are churned out of the system based on the fantasy that these two humanities are one and will continue as currently constituted.

We need a blend of the two, such that the useful theories and methods of each percolate into the other. We need Humanities Three. It will appeal to the politics and ideals of those opposed to neoliberalism, even as it will be attractive to students who have been driven to instrumentalism by the weight of student loans and the threat of precarious employment.

To give an idea of what this *rapprochement* would look like, here is an imaginary set of queries to pose to traditional literary scholars (actually, to any literary scholar) and new communications faculty (a few of whom will actually know the answers):

- how many texts (books, movie tickets, online rentals, games) are sold in the countries they study;

- how many people buy or borrow texts each year, and what proportion read virtual or material versions;

- which companies dominate cultural production and why;

- how many such corporations are there now versus ten or twenty years ago; and

- what empirical research is available on forms of reading, playing, and viewing texts?

Can they explain:

- the business structure of the culture industries;

- the experience of working in them as a forester, designer, or driver;

- the relationships between novelists, agents, and editors;

- how books appear in the front of chain stores (or are never in stock);

- the role of the International Publishers Association, the Pan African Booksellers Association, the Book Industry Study Group, the Publishers Database for Responsible and Ethical Paper Sourcing, the Federation of Indian Publishers, the Federation of European Publishers, the Society of Publishers in Asia, and the Book Industry Environmental Council—or their equivalents in other sectors;

- cultural policies affecting publishers and libraries; and

- the relative environmental impact of ebooks versus paper books and online searches versus air travel?

These ecomaterialist principles can percolate through Humanities Three, offering students the answers to questions from beyond the traditional cloisters—but also beyond the myopia of neoliberalism.

Notes

1. The references backing up the data used in this piece can be found in Toby Miller, *Blow Up the Humanities* (Philadelphia, PA: Temple University Press, 2012).

2. Meera Louis, "$1 Trillion Debt Crushes Business Dreams of U.S. Students," Bloomberg Business, June 6, 2013, accessed March 1, 2016, http://www.bloomberg.com/news/articles/2013-06-06/-1-trillion-debt-crushes-business-dreams-of-u-s-students.

3. William Harms, "Gary S. Becker, Nobel-Winning Scholar of Economics and Sociology, 1930–2014," UChicago News, May 4, 2014, accessed March 1, 2016, http://news.uchicago.edu/article/2014/05/04/gary-s-becker-nobel-winning-scholar-economics-and-sociology-1930-2014.

4. The White House, "The Recovery Act," accessed March 1, 2016, https://www.whitehouse.gov/recovery.

5. The White House, "Remarks by the President in State of Union Address," January 25, 2011, accessed March 1, 2016, https://www.whitehouse.gov/the-press-office/2011/01/25/remarks-president-state-union-address.

6. John Strausbaugh, "Eggheads' Naughty Word Games," *New York Times*, December 27, 2004, accessed March 1, 2016, http://www.nytimes.com/2004/12/27/books/eggheads-naughty-word-games.html?_r=0.

27

Neoliberalism and the End of Education

Michael Wayne

The neoliberal paradigm died *economically* in the 2008 crash, the consequences and fallout of which we are still living with, as wages and standards of living continue to free-fall. But *ideologically* the neoliberal paradigm remains as strong as ever. As various commentators have noted, this is 'zombie capitalism'[1]: dead, yet still very active, cannibalizing what is left of social wealth and public resources. Education is a key example of this. David Willetts, former Minister of State for Universities and Science exemplified the Demolition Government's wilful institutional vandalism by building on New Labour's neoliberal initiatives and moving over wholly to a tuition fees system for university funding. This has given neoliberalism the economic underpinning for a tremendous ideological re-functioning of the purposes of higher education. The values or ideology of entrepreneurialism are now coursing through the HE system. Yet the gulf between words and the reality of an economically dying paradigm shows itself constantly. Entrepreneurialism— which sounds dynamic, active, and wealth creating—has come to mean for more and more people self-employed, insecure work—often in the personal services sector. Even within the terms of capitalist economic activity—this hardly counts as value producing activity—it merely counts as people surviving off the disposable incomes of others.

Ideology necessarily corrupts the meaning of words and the implications for an education system that has those words forced down its throat, is profound. The corruption of the meaning of words is a necessary consequence of an economy as skewed towards the elites as our broken economy is. Take the traditional Enlightenment liberal virtues of tolerance, diversity, equality, and reason as an example. Initially neoliberalism did not need liberalism, while liberalism regarded neoliberalism (or Thatcherism as it was then known) with horror. But by the 1990s, in order to secure itself, neoliberalism had to tilt from brute coercion and start to reproduce itself with a greater role for consent. Liberalism was to become a key ideological resource in this, fashioning a rapprochement for liberalism with the new rising power of capital. In the United Kingdom this transformed the political culture of both the Labour Party and the Conservative Party, as embodied in their leaders, Tony Blair and David Cameron. As Slavoj Žižek noted,[2] multiculturalism became the logic of late capitalism. The openly reactionary values of racism, sexism, homophobia, and xenophobia exemplified by Thatcherism, were to be officially replaced with public commitments to equality and diversity in order to integrate significant sources of discontent into the neoliberal framework. The extent for example to which young black people have been weaned away from an earlier politics of radical anti-racism, anti-imperialism, and anti-capitalism, in favour of entrepreneurialism, suggests that this second phase of culturally progressive neoliberalism has not been without its successes.

Liberalism's traditional commitment to the virtues of education were similarly appropriated by the neoliberals. Tony Blair made education one of his key policy areas along with his special advisor, Andrew—subsequently Lord—Adonis. Education was to be the driver of social inclusion—but it turned out that inclusion meant the entrance into education of private providers, such as the Harris Academies (run by Philip—subsequently Lord—Harris, a carpet salesman) that now controls thirty-five primary and secondary schools in South East London. The scramble for Academies is about establishing market share before they are finally transformed from their non-profit charity status—from which huge salaries to senior managers can still be leveraged by top slicing tax-payer money per student enrolled—into fully-fledged profit-driven operations. Thus education goes the way of other public services and becomes a source of revenue for an increasingly rent-seeking, parasitic capitalism that in the United Kingdom especially, has little commitment to invest in the productive sector.

What happens to the liberal notion of advancement through education when the economy is skewed around a low-wage, low-skill service sector for the 'proles' and for the professionals, financial services, real estate, and advertising—jobs that all require a fair degree of institutionalised lying? What happens is that advancement through education becomes itself a lie—except for the elites who enter the top jobs through the nexus of private schools and 'Oxbridge', and go onto dominate the state apparatus, business sector, and the media. A report[3] by the Commission on Social Mobility and Poverty, chaired by arch-Blairite MP Alan Milburn, recognised the domination of the elites through the channel of education. For example the report found that while only 7 per cent of the population have attended private schools, 71 per cent of senior judges, 62 per cent of the armed forces, 50 per cent of the House of Lords, 44 per cent of creatives in the film, TV, and music industry, 43 per cent of newspaper columnists, and 26 per cent of BBC executives, have been to private schools. But while liberalism in the political sphere can diagnose a problem, it cannot recognise that the source of the problem derives from the inevitable inequalities generated by a failing economic model (capitalism), still less formulate solutions to those problems, since that would inevitably mean encroaching on the prerogatives of private property and the market.

If education is working well for the elites, the prescriptions for making it work well for the majority become more desperate, more colonised by the logic that causes the problems in the first place. Within education, 'employability' for the majority who do not benefit from the networks of privilege, is becoming an increasingly prevalent pressure, threatening to transform the curriculum according to what business-minded educationalists think business wants or needs. The employability agenda can seek to do no more than equip students to compete more effectively with each other. It cannot change the ratio between graduates seeking graduate-level jobs and actual jobs available. Only cutting the number of people going to universities can do that—a regressive measure—or allocating greater investment—both public and private—into the economy, including the social economy. The latter though requires a confrontation with capital and its vast hording of wealth in the banking and financial system, whose autonomy from public and democratic accountability is fiercely defended.

Capitalism's need for universal and high quality education is very likely in terminal decline. The lack of investment in the productive economy shows that the mainspring of capital responsible for allocation and accumulation is busted. New technology will continue to displace jobs and there is growing awareness that the next wave of AI technology will wipe out many middle-class jobs.[4] Globalisation will continue to push capital eastwards in search of profits from cheap labour. But the clock is ticking. Labour in the East will gradually make the same claims on capital that made labour in the West unaffordable.

Already there are signs that capitalism with Chinese characteristics is accelerating through the stages of Western capitalism, and having gone through the period of primitive accumulation, the industrial workshop of the world, is now hitting a wall. Where can capital go next? Capital has always relied on 'spatial fixes' for its problem of surplus capital,[5] but unless capital finds a vast new surplus of exploitable labour on the moon, space and time is running out. What will happen to democracy as capitalism becomes more cornered, less able to find escape routes? Will the era of Western liberal democratic capitalism come to an end and converge with the more dictatorial models of capitalism that have flourished in Latin America and Asia? Let us hope that enough people get access to sources of *critical* education—that might now migrate away from the formal schooling/university system—to not only diagnose the problems down to their roots, but also to offer solutions outside the framework of private ownership of social wealth. Then words and education will mean something once again.

Notes

1. Chris Harman, *Zombie Capitalism: Global Crisis and the Relevance of Marx* (London: Bookmarks, 2009).

2. Slavoj Žižek, "Multiculturalism, or, the Cultural Logic of Multinational Capitalism," *New Left Review* 225 (1997): 28–51.

3. Alan Milburn, *Elitist Britain?*, accessed 1 March 2016, https://www.gov.uk/government/uploads/system/uploads/attachment_data/file/347915/Elitist_Britain_-_Final.pdf.

4. Randall Collins, "The End of Middle-Class Work: No More Escapes," in *Does Capitalism Have a Future?*, eds. Immanuel Wallerstein et al. (Oxford: Oxford University Press, 2013), 37–70.

5. David Harvey, *The New Imperialism* (Oxford: Oxford University Press, 2003), 88–89.

28

Freedom of Speech Is Always under Attack in Privileged White Man Land

Howard Littler

Most people agree that no one should face violence or imprison-ment for the opinions they spout, no matter how boneheaded. However, coming up with an adequate understanding of what freedom of speech politically means today is a little more com-plicated. In fact, it is a quagmire of open-ended questions about power, context, and ethics that raise a series of 'yes it's legal, but is it right?' quandaries. To sidestep this is to pretend that we are all, together with Richard Dawkins, living in a permanent debating chamber in which all ideas get the same exposure, all are equal, and where a grasp of logic and reason are the only advantages. We're not quite there yet.

Students' unions are the latest threat to this beautiful lib-eral utopia. 'This is a big day in the fight for free speech on cam-pus', roared *Spiked* in 2015, announcing the release of their 'Free Speech University Rankings'.[1] My own students' union, Gold-smiths, is ranked 'red' in their traffic light barometer and we are seen as 'hostile to free speech and free expression'. Our policies on supporting a woman's right to choose, our commitment to proactively tackling 'lad culture', and our opposition to providing platforms for fascists contribute to this low mark. The ranking came in the same week that *Spiked* claimed that we banned a comedian. No policy exists to ban any comedian and she was in fact cancelled by the Comedy Society but don't let that get in the way of three whole days of free publicity.

Other recent controversies have included students' unions nightclubs taking Robin Thicke's *Blurred Lines* off of their playlists for its anti-feminist reading of sexual consent. For this they were pilloried in the media by outraged columnists.[2]

At the heart of this analysis is a misconception about what students' unions are that needs addressing. As fundamentally membership organisations, policies are regularly debated and democratically decided. The venues we run are essentially private members clubs—so why then shouldn't students decide who is and who is not welcome? Why shouldn't our members have a say on what is sold in our shop or what music is played in our nightclubs?

The greatest quality of students' unions as campaigning organisations is their disposition to challenge the status quo, to go beyond talking about problems as students in the lecture theatre, and to have a go tackling them. This means they will often be environments where the rights of minority groups are more advanced than in wider society, such as the policy of having gender neutral toilets and using correct gender pronouns, both derided by *Spiked*.

It's no coincidence that the likes of Goldsmiths, SOAS, Edinburgh, and LSE all get a disapproving red next to their names in the *Spiked* list. They are widely regarded as some of the most vocal politically. This doesn't just go against the libertarian tastes of the people at *Spiked*. Since John Major's government passed the 1994 Education Act, students' unions come under the remit of the Charity Commission, which makes it easier for people who have politically lost an argument to weaponise charity law against campaigning unions and to argue that their work on social justice is ultra vires. But aren't going against the grain, challenging power, and turning social norms upside down not the very epitome of what a true commitment to freedom of speech might look like?

The reductionist opportunism of *Spiked*'s interpretation of freedom of speech is no clearer than when Edinburgh University Students' Association's (EUSA) policy of inclusion of trans students is cited as a supposed attack on dearly-held liberties. In what alternative reality is requiring students to recognise the sexual identity of transgender students viewed as negative?[3]

It is obvious that *Spiked* has a very particular utopia. It refers to a privileged white man's land where fascists are welcome on campus to intimidate non-white students, and where anti-abortion activists are free to hand out pictures of foetuses and propaganda calling those who have had abortions baby-killers and making women generally feel uncomfortable in what is supposed to be their space of study.

If it wouldn't make me the least popular person in the office tomorrow, I would invite *Spiked* writers to attend a Goldsmiths Students Assembly, the beating heart of students' union policy making. Open disagreement is rife, continuous, and encouraged. The same goes for our debating society where, in recent meetings, we have discussed Israel and Palestine, the Prophet Mohammed cartoons, and the *Sun*'s Page 3.

Let's also not forget what is omitted from this analysis. There is no criticism of universities bringing police on campus to spray students with CS gas for protesting peacefully and no reference to the injunctions served against them, which meant, in some cases, that students could not even enter their own campuses. Isn't that a bigger threat to freedom of speech in universities than well-intentioned policy against playing a song that boasts about blurring the lines of sexual consent?

If the *Spiked* writers paused for one second from their Pub Landlord routine on political correctness (or institutionalised politeness, as comedian Stewart Lee calls it[4]), they may even notice a genuine and real threat to freedom of speech on the horizon in the form of the Counter-Terrorism and Security Bill, which embeds suspicion into our universities and turns academic staff into part-time spies for the state, trained to keep an eye out for anyone who says anything remotely radical. In the government's *Prevent* Strategy document they list indicators of 'radicalism' or 'extremism' to include 'a need for identity, meaning and belonging' and 'a desire for political or moral change.'[5] I think on those grounds you'd need a whole government department dealing with just Goldsmiths.

It is clear how *Spiked* and their counterparts want to envision students' unions: as never ending debating chambers, welcoming with open arms the bigots and fascists we campaign against and rejecting a collectivism that is uncomfortable with their idea of the status quo. Their version of free speech—that it is a neutral, black-and-white concept—is politically charged and discourages challenging authority. Not only is this intensely boring, but it's dangerous, and should be rejected.

Notes

1. Tom Slater, "Exposed: The Staggering Scale of Censorship on Campus," *Spiked*, February 3, 2015, accessed March 7, 2016, http://www.spiked-online .com/newsite/article/exposed-the-staggering-scale-of-censorship-on-campus/ 16658#.Vt2Dn0sQfHg.
2. For example, Brendan O'Neill, "Trouble on Campus: The Rise of Ban-Happy Student Leaders," *Daily Telegraph*, October 31, 2015, accessed March 7, 2016, http://www.telegraph.co.uk/education/universityeducation/11658770/ Trouble-on-campus-the-rise-of-ban-happy-student-leaders.html.
3. Gavin Dewar, "Edinburgh University Receives 'Red' Free Speech Ranking," *Student Newspaper*, February 10, 2015, accessed March 7, 2016, http://www .studentnewspaper.org/edinburgh-university-receives-red-free-speech-ranking.
4. "Stewart Lee on Political Correctness," YouTube video, 2:01, from a performance broadcasted by BBC Radio 4 on May 16, 2007, posted by "Dave Powell," August 9, 2007, https://www.youtube.com/watch?v=1IYx4Bc6_eE.
5. HM Government, "Channel: Vulnerability Assessment Framework," October 2012, accessed March 7, 2016, https://www.gov.uk/government/uploads/ system/uploads/attachment_data/file/118187/vul-assessment.pdf.

29

Prevent Education?

Jonathan Rosenhead

Some issues pass through many organs of the body politic like a barium meal, rendering visible flaws and faults that might otherwise escape detection. Israel–Palestine is one of them. In this account of the impact of the UK government's *Prevent* strategy on education in general and higher education in particular, the Israel–Palestine issue will highlight the guts of the issue.

Prevent now has a more than ten-year history, initially as a voluntary programme. It began to attract the more searching scrutiny in 2014, when the government decided to give it statutory teeth, a proposal that became law the following year. But even under the preceding voluntary regime, many of the practices implemented by and within universities under its influence had already had a chilling effect on the opportunities for debate within the student body.

Consider Freshers' Week at Lancaster University in 2014. The student union president was startled to receive a text message that police were photographing two posters in her office window. One said 'Not for Shale', the other: 'End Israel's attacks on Gaza'. A union officer who asked the police for an explanation was told that 'I was potentially committing a public order offence.' Really? Public order offences range from riot and violent disorder through affray and harassment through to threatening abusive or insulting behaviour. 'I felt like the whole incident was an intimidation tactic', the president told a journalist.[1]

These practices stem from the political atmosphere engendered since 2006 by the Home Office programme, *Prevent Violent Extremism*. Its rationale has centred on the vague, conveniently elastic concept of 'non-violent extremism'. Ideas seemingly qualify as 'non-violent extremism', even if violence is not even advocated, if they are judged capable of generating a climate that could lead vulnerable individuals to carry out violent acts in the future. This is known as the conveyor-belt model.[2] Prime Minister David Cameron has put it succinctly: 'No-one becomes a terrorist from a standing start.'[3] That is, people become terrorists gradually, and anything that could start the journey has to be 'prevented'. This rationale has motivated a systematic search for and surveillance of potential 'non-violent extremism' throughout the United Kingdom, but especially in Muslim communities and student Islamic societies.

As the *Prevent* programme eventually defined extremism, it meant hostility to 'British values', which in turn are characterised as: 'democracy, rule of law, equality of opportunity, freedom of speech and the rights of all men and women to live free from persecution of any kind.'[4] This definition conflates universal human values with those of Britain (whose foreign policy in any case regularly contradicts them). In people's experience of the *Prevent* programme, any Muslim in particular who highlights this inconsistency, or who criticises particular aspects of foreign policy, is all too open to labelling as an extremist.[5]

Turning Prevent into a Duty

The rationale for the wider anti-terror legislative framework, including the *Prevent* programme, came from the security establishment—which tends of course to favour the extension of its own powers. The potential for muting criticism must surely have been an attractive feature for ministers. But there was another self-interest of politicians that, since the 7/7 bombings in 2005, has pointed in the same direction. Given that another atrocity will almost certainly happen (like the 1930s dictum that 'the bomber will always get through') no government dares to run the risk of refusing the police and spooks a power that it could subsequently be claimed would have prevented the carnage.

There was, however, far less enthusiasm for the original *Prevent* programme among the professional staff tasked with implementing it in public-sector institutions. Teachers and lecturers did not embrace the approach with requisite enthusiasm, so its coverage was quite patchy. The government's response was to put the *Prevent* programme on a statutory basis, requiring all public-sector institutions to implement it. Its Counter-Terrorism and Security Bill included a section, Part 5, on The Risk of People Being Drawn into Terrorism. This section proposed to 'create a duty for specified bodies to have due regard, in the exercise of their functions, to the need to prevent people from being drawn into terrorism', by following government guidance.[6]

The formerly quasi-voluntary cooperation would now become a legally enforceable duty. There would be a legal obligation on public servants (especially teachers and lecturers, but also doctors, social workers, etc.,) to inform the police about any person who may be en route to 'radicalisation', or expresses 'extremist' views. Public institutions would need to monitor such views and report them to Home Office representatives, who were to be embedded in local authorities and police forces.

The inclusion of the United Kingdom's universities within the remit of this legislation generated the most strenuous opposition, some of it from surprising quarters. Forthright critics included Lord Butler of Brockwell, who had been head of the Civil Service for ten years, Lady Manningham-Buller, Director General of MI5 for five years, and Lord MacDonald, Director of Public Prosecutions from 2003–2008. All concurred that the proposal went too far towards limiting free speech. It would contradict the duty on universities to protect free speech; it would turn universities into 'places of surveillance'; and it would supposedly protect our values by suppressing views rather than debating them, an effect directly contrary to those values.

According to Oxford academic Karma Nabulsi, the Bill itself was extremist in the name of security—more dangerous indeed than 1950s McCarthyism.[7] Previously, regardless of people's general views on free speech, there had been a broad consensus that any constraints on universities should remain light, in order to protect scholarship and the education of the next generation. But no longer.

The Slippery Slope

The political effects of this *glissando* down the slippery slope towards systematic surveillance show up with particular clarity on Israel–Palestine. This issue sits astride a fault line testing our belief that we live in a fundamentally liberal country. There has long been an entrenched support for (and unwillingness to criticise) Israel, stretching most way across the country's institutions and political parties. Yet within civil society, not just in Britain but across Europe, Israel consistently rates alongside Iran, Pakistan, and North Korea as the countries whose global influence is most negative.[8]

The West's complicity with Israel's war crimes is certainly prominent in the minds of many young UK Muslims, and with some reason. So perhaps one can never start too young in detecting thought crimes. Could that have been the rationale for the police questioning a London schoolboy in summer 2015 about the 'terrorist-like' views expressed in leaflets he had brought to school? He was also told that the badges he wore were 'extremist'. But the badges just said 'Free Palestine', and the leaflets promoted the entirely non-violent boycott of Israel. The boy was told that his tutor had a legal duty to report such views to the police.[9] Teachers and students have reported many comparable cases. This is what happens when the concept of individuals 'vulnerable to radicalisation' and requiring 'safeguarding' measures to protect them and others is operationalised by an attentive state machine.

Over recent years university events have frequently been monitored for 'extremist' views, even before the passing of the 2015 Counter-Terrorism and Security Act. A prominent case was a conference on Institutional Islamophobia due to be held at Birkbeck College in December 2014. Birkbeck cancelled the booking at only a few days' notice—on 'security' grounds, and on the proposal of Camden Council's *Prevent* officers. The Charity Commission too has been implementing the *Prevent* programme within universities. Student union officers have reported having lengthy, intimidating meetings with the commission, who asked probing questions about the Islamic as well as Palestine societies, and even about 'Save our NHS'.[10] Student groups have been denied room bookings for meetings to discuss the *Prevent* programme itself, as well as the Israel–Palestine issue. Abject compliance has many examples: the British Library declined an offer to archive Taliban documents, for fear that staff might be arrested or prosecuted for terrorism[11] and a Muslim student who read a book on terrorism was accused of being a potential terrorist.[12]

The view of Sir Peter Fahy, chief constable of Greater Manchester police, who speaks for the police on the *Prevent* strategy, is forthright. The thrust of government policy is misguided and indeed counterproductive at a time when Muslims in the United Kingdom feel increasingly alienated: 'There is a concern that efforts to control extremist narratives will limit free speech and backfire if we don't get the balance right. The efforts to control extremism and limit protest by those caught by too wide a definition may undermine the very rights and British values you seek to protect.'[13] Meanwhile any students who might become protojihadis will continue meeting each other at suitable venues on and off campus, while liberal Britain erodes from the inside.

Conflicts over Implementation

The proposal to shift from the voluntary scheme to a statutory basis provoked opposition from the relevant trade unions, whose conferences have denounced the *Prevent* programme[14] or have explicitly supported a boycott.[15] The National Union of Students (NUS) also decided on a boycott—for example by refusing cooperation with university administrations. According to a study of public-sector staff practices, a false sense of expertise—instilled in them partly by *Prevent* training—'has resulted in massive over-referrals' to the compulsory 'deradicalisation' sessions of the 'Channel' programme; 80 per cent are 'deemed unworthy of any follow-up.'[16] The NUS campaign *Preventing Prevent*, sees the government measures as 'looking to force PREVENT into every aspect of our lives and society' and the NUS itself has adopted as its slogan 'Students Not Suspects.'[17]

Despite such widespread opposition and authoritative, damaging critiques, the roll-out of the programme has proceeded. Implementation has several components. First, each institution is required to train staff in monitoring and countering any signs of 'extremism'. Second, each staff member has a reporting duty on suspect individuals. Third, 'vulnerable' students may be referred to the Channel programme. While these practices are mandated by legislation, compliance is reinforced by fear at all levels—fear that institutions may be penalised, or that individuals' careers may be jeopardised, by inadequate compliance. And students certainly fear that penalties will be imposed if they refuse 'deradicalisation' sessions.

The *Prevent* programme has thus been cleverly designed for routine implementation. Institutions and individuals get drawn into its clockwork mechanism, unless there is both principled opposition and group solidarity. It is not necessary for anyone involved to accept its underlying conveyor-belt model, nor to believe that it will do anything to avert terrorism. Does even the government really believe this?

For all those reasons, professional staff in a variety of institutions are now under pressure to search for, detect, and report as 'extremism' what in most cases will be the expression of politically and morally-based views. The ensuing conflicts will shape the prospects for defending free expression and open debate in universities.

Notes

1. Louise Tickle, "Anti-Terror Bill: Making Radical Ideas a Crime on Campus," *Guardian*, December 2, 2014, accessed March 1 2016, http://www.theguardian .com/education/2014/dec/02/anti-terror-bill-making-radical-ideas -crime-campus.

2. Marc Sageman, *Leaderless Jihad: Terror Networks in the Twenty-First Century* (Philadelphia: University of Pennsylvania Press, 2008).

3. BBC News, "Cameron Unveils Strategy to Tackle Islamist Extremism," July 20, 2015, accessed March 1, 2016, http://www.bbc.co.uk/news/uk-33590305.

4. Home Office, *Prevent Strategy*, Cm 8092 (London: HMSO 2011) 34.

5. See Arun Kundnani, *Spooked: How Not to Prevent Violent Extremism* (London: Institute of Race Relations, 2009); Jahangir Mohammed and Adnan Siddiqui, *The PREVENT Strategy: A Cradle to Grave Police-State* (London: Cage, 2013).

6. Counter-Terrorism and Security Bill, H.C. 127, Session 2014–15 (November 26, 2014), accessed March 1, 2016, http://www.publications.parliament.uk/ pa/bills/cbill/2014-2015/0127/en/15127en.htm.

7. Karma Nabulsi, "Theresa May's Prevent Bill Is Extremism in the Name of Security," *Guardian*, February 4, 2015, accessed March 1, 2016, http://www .theguardian.com/commentisfree/2015/feb/04/theresa-may-prevent-bill -extremism-security-terrorism.

8. BBC News, "Russian Image Has Deteriorated – BBC World Service Poll," June 4, 2014, accessed March 1 2016, http://www.bbc.co.uk/news/27685494.

9. Simon Hooper, "Stifling Freedom of Expression in UK Schools', July 23, 2015, accessed March 1 2016, http://www.aljazeera.com/indepth/features/2015/07/ stifling-freedom-expression-uk-schools-150721080612049.html.

10. Malia Bouattia ed., *Preventing PREVENT: A Student Handbook on Countering the PREVENT Agenda on Campus* (London: National Union of Students, 2015) 31; National Union of Students, "Preventing PREVENT Handbooks," *NSU Connect*, February 12, 2015, accessed March 1 2016, http:// www.nusconnect.org.uk/articles/preventing-prevent-handbooks.

11. Katy Sian, "How Do You Spot a Student Extremist in A University?," *Guardian*, July 21, 2015, accessed March 1, 2016, http://www.theguardian .com/higher-education-network/2015/jul/21/how-do-you-spot-a-student -extremist-in-a-university.

12. Randeep Ramesh and Josh Halliday, "Student Accused of Being a Terrorist for Reading Book on Terrorism," *Guardian*, September 24, 2015, accessed March 1, 2016, http://www.theguardian.com/education/2015/sep/24/ student-accused-being-terrorist-reading-book-terrorism.

13. Vikram Dodd and Alan Travis, "Anti-Extremism Drive Puts British Values at Risk, Says Police Chief," *Guardian*, October 19, 2015, accessed March 1, 2016, http://www.theguardian.com/uk-news/2015/oct/19/government-extremism -crackdown-hurt-uk-values-peter-fahy-manchester.

14. For example, the National Union of Teachers.

15. University and College Union, Prevent Agenda: Conference Motion, accessed March 1, 2016, http://www.ucu.org.uk/index.cfm?articleid=7523#62.

16. Malia Bouattia ed., *Preventing PREVENT*, 15.

17. NUS Black Students' Campaign, December 2, 2015, accessed September 8, 2016, https://www.facebook.com/nusBSC/posts/10153474899973197; National Union of Students, accessed March 1, 2016, https://www.facebook .com/events/1487881704845683.

30

Social Science Inc.

John Holmwood

The politics of austerity in the aftermath of the financial crisis of 2008 and the election of the Conservative-led coalition government in 2010 produced drastic cuts to public spending. It has involved the reassertion of neoliberal policies whose application to the financial sector had created the crisis in the first place. One consequence is the dismantling of public higher education in England, with the removal of all direct funding of undergraduate degree programmes in arts, humanities, and the social sciences and the creation of a supposed 'level-playing field' to allow for-profit providers to compete for students.[1]

This has led to the dramatic attenuation of the democratic functions of universities and consolidated the growth of a neo-liberal knowledge regime marked by increased managerialism, the growth of an 'audit culture' and performance management of teaching and research. In a new competitive environment, the university is seen by its managers as a 'brand' to be promoted and protected. For the most part, attention has been on the consequences for teaching—the transformation of students into consumers[2]—and the external assessment of research: game playing in the Research Excellence Framework[3] and the displacement of the substance of research into the maximisation of scores on performance indicators of excellence and impact.

But something else is now emerging as part of this neoliberal knowledge regime, namely, the brand management and incorporation of social science itself. This is evident in a recent report, *The Business of People* produced in 2015 by the Campaign for Social Science.[4] The Campaign was initiated by the Academy of Social Sciences, which is made up of 1000 fellows and 47 member learned societies (part of what the report calls the 'soft power' of Britain), in turn encompassing 90,000 social scientists. Just how does it represent the social sciences and whose values does it promote?

The report is overwhelmingly instrumental and, as it states in the foreword, is designed to appeal to the 'Treasury, ministers, MPs and policy makers'. Its focus on policymakers and practitioners is unremitting: 'Advancing and applying science depends on profits, policies, markets, organisations, and attitudes.' The attitudes of the public, on the other hand, are presented as potential obstacles to policy objectives. For example, it argues that 'study of public values and attitudes is vital, too, especially when innovation prompts uncertainties and concerns, as with genetically modified crops or shale gas extraction.'[5] And it warns that 'without a better grasp of *people*, technological advances may be frustrated or blocked, and fail to realise their potential.'[6]

The report emphasises interdisciplinary approaches and returns frequently to this topic. In a separate comment in response to criticisms of the report, the director of the Campaign has stated that the report does not specify particular modes of interdisciplinarity, but that they could include 'critical

sociologists working with anthropologists, philosophers working with synthetic biologists, educationalists working with neu-
roscientists, or historians working with political scientists.'[7] In
nearly all instances, however, what is emphasised is links across
the social sciences, natural sciences, and engineering, or across
bio-sciences and social sciences. Indeed, its call for a 10 per
cent increase in funding in real terms is specifically attached
to interdisciplinary research in social sciences, natural sciences,
and engineering. Only one reference is made to the humanities,
but, once again, it is the indispensability of cross-disciplinary,
'problem-focussed' research[8] that is stressed, as it is in all cases.
Towards the end of the report it seems to belie this dominant
emphasis by defining the social sciences as 'disciplined curiosity', but immediately this is qualified as '*applied* curiosity'.

The language of the report is a particularly narrow version
of the impact agenda where all publicly-funded research is to
have users in mind, with commercial beneficiaries, policy makers, and practitioners foremost. Researchers are recommended
to engage with potential users at the earliest stages of research,
including that of its design and seek to maximise its subsequent
impact with them. This is what makes research 'problem-focussed', where just what constitutes a problem should be co-
defined with users.

This undermines both the critical functions of research
and its independence. Research councils like the Economic
and Social Research Council (ESRC) are increasingly setting
research priorities determined by the Department for Business,
Innovation and Science that provides its block grant of funding—for example, on big data or the application of neurosci-
ence to social problems. This is also evident in steered calls for
grant applications and also specific co-funding of projects like

the What Works Centres. Independence has become narrowed to mean simply that research bids are peer-reviewed only from the perspective of their academic excellence. However, the latter includes review of their 'pathways to impact' and, for large grants and centres bids, this will include user representatives. Where government is a user, this may involve a representative from the Department for Business, Innovation and Science on the evaluation panel, especially in the case of applications for large grants and centres.

At the same time, under the dictates of audit culture and its performance indicators, individual universities are increasingly matching these research priorities to their own research strategies. The pursuit of knowledge is replaced by the pursuit of grants. With individual academics and departments evaluated according to their grant capture, this has increased the number of applications made for funding, thereby creating various measures of demand management. Research is shaped and managed by universities and research councils alike, and all are converging on the same problems and topics as the ESRC steers. This is so notwithstanding the ESRC's continuing stated commitment to 'responsive mode' funding—university research strategies constrain the responses of their staff within their own similar research priorities. This bureaucratisation of research is accompanied by the language of 'innovation', 'transformation', and 'disruption'— familiar tropes of neoliberal discourse—but rather belied by the nature of how research agendas are set. What is preferred is research directed at behaviours, rather than at social structures.

What is striking about the report is that it comes in the wake of the publication of Thomas Piketty's *Capital in the Twenty-First Century*,[9] documenting the rise in inequality in Western countries over the last decades. This found its way into the mainstream media, as well as in reports by agencies such as OECD. Yet structured social inequality is not mentioned at all in the report, nor is race and ethnicity, or any other research on social structure. These profoundly affect the circumstances of people's lives, yet all the report has to say about them are their derived consequences in terms of people's attitudes and behaviours and how those may be a problem for policy makers and practitioners in attaining their objectives.

Sometimes the report refers to social divisions and social structures by coded references to the 'context' of policy and practice. They are also implied by the report's concern that investments in social science data, such as the birth cohort study and longitudinal studies, should be maintained. These are an important source of information about social structures and the report also seeks increased investment in big data and administrative data, including the recommendation of a 'statutory presumption in sharing de-identified public (administrative) data for research processes'.

Yet while the commercial significance of big data is stressed throughout the report, it is silent about the fact that commercial interest in such data includes the evaluation of policy and performance (including that of academics themselves through academic analytics and the possible metricisation of the REF), where the mixed data sets and algorithms associated with commercial applied data science become proprietary products and, therefore, not themselves available for critical scrutiny. The report says nothing about the critical functions of social science at the same time as it opens the door to the privatisation and commercialisation of those critical functions.

Occasionally in the report, the facade cracks and the real substance of what is at issue in this and any election can be glimpsed. Thus, it remarks that, 'growth is not given or necessarily consensual' and goes on to say that 'choices must be made, about the balance of public and private, taxation and spending, freedom and constraint and about where and to whose benefit. Social science supplies context and helps us locate ourselves.'[10] Precious little, however, is said about how social science addresses context, or how sustained research on context could be consistent with the impact agenda or the report's own 'problem-focussed' orientation. Nor does the report locate its own plea for funding in the 'balance of public and private, taxation and spending.'

Within sociology, this raises a familiar question asked by Howard Becker[11]: 'whose side are we on?' His was not an argument for partisan social science, but rather involved the observation that any social science that took seriously the circumstances and attitudes of the disadvantaged would be seen as partisan, simply by virtue of accounting for their views. As Becker observed, a social science that addressed the interests of those in subordinate positions would also appear unrespectable and partisan, while that which addressed the powerful would appear respectable and cloaked in objectivity. However, it was an objectivity that derived simply from the naturalisation of power relations, not from being outside them.

In this context, both the report and the associated Campaign for the Social Sciences are not simply naive; they are also calculating and hierarchical. The report presents itself as the protector of social science and the promoter of its interests at the same time as it presents a partial picture of them and displaces the commitments of those it enjoins to show solidarity. Critics like myself are accused of risking the future funding of the social sciences[12] by our 'divisiveness' and, thereby, also risking the futures of early-career researchers. This pressure is similar to managerial pressure within the university not to disrupt the brand. Suppose the government does not accept the claim for extra funding, it is likely, nonetheless, to accept the steer toward interdisciplinary research across the social sciences, natural sciences, and engineering, and the emphasis on behavioural change. And this will have consequences for the careers of social scientists that do not share these orientations.

Were the situation not so serious, it might be thought of as a version of *Fawlty Towers,* where, in the run-up to an election, social scientists are told: 'don't mention the politics'. But, if there are choices about the public and the private, and about taxation and spending, to be made, we should remember that choices can arise without them necessarily being put to the electorate. Indeed, this is, for elites, the preferred way to proceed. So, after the last election, direct public funding of undergraduate degree programmes was removed and replaced by fees, despite not being put to the electorate. An 82 per cent cut in public spending was achieved at the same time as greater revenue for universities was raised from student indebtedness. Yet, successive British Social Attitudes reports have showed the public both to be opposed to student debt (at levels lower than was subsequently introduced) and to believe that university education is about far more than instrumental purposes. The only decline in support for publicly-funded higher education is among those with graduate-level qualifications (themselves the beneficiaries of the previous system).

Just as university leaders have been willing to compromise the values of higher education in return for money from student fees, so the authors of *The Business of People* are willing to compromise the values of social science for money. Should we be surprised that the transformation of the university under neo-liberal policies of marketisation should also have their impact on the configuration of its disciplines? We shouldn't be: funding comes at a price. Nevertheless, when in the pursuit of public money, shouldn't there be more critical attention devoted in social science research to those issues that plague our societies rather than those that have been mobilised to accommodate the interests of elites?

Notes

1. John Holmwood, "From Social Rights to the Market: Neoliberalism and the Knowledge Economy," *International Journal of Lifelong Education* 33, no. 1 (2014): 62–76. doi:10.1080/02601370.2013.873213.

2. Stefan Collini, *What Are Universities For?* (London: Penguin Books, 2012).

3. Derek Sayer, *Rank Hypocrisies: The Insult of the REF* (London: Sage Swifts, 2015).

4. Campaign for Social Science, *The Business of People: The Significance of Social Science over the Next Decade* (London: Sage, 2015), accessed March 1, 2016, https://campaignforsocialscience.org.uk/wp-content/uploads/2015/02/Business-of-People-Full-Report.pdf.

5. Ibid., 6.

6. Ibid., 5.

7. James Wilsdon, March 14, 2015, comment on John Holmwood, "Social Scientists Shouldn't Shy Away from Political Debates," *Guardian*, March 12, 2015, accessed March 1, 2016, https://www.theguardian.com/higher-education-network/2015/mar/12/social-scientists-shouldnt-shy-away-from-political-debates#comment-48894966.

8. Campaign for Social Science, *The Business of People*, 7.

9. Thomas Piketty, *Capital in the Twenty-First Century* (Cambridge, MA: The Belknap Press of Harvard University Press, 2014).

10. Campaign for Social Science, *The Business of People*, 8.

11. Howard S. Becker, "Whose Side Are We On?" *Social Problems* 14, no. 3 (1967): 239–47. doi:10.2307/799147.

12. James Wilsdon, comment on John Holmwood.

31

The Strange Death of the Liberal University

Michael Bailey

strange/streɪn(d)ʒ: unusual or surprising; difficult to understand or explain: *politicians have some strange ideas about what universities are for | this new breed of university managers are strange fish indeed | how strange that most academics acquiesced to the marketisation of universities.*

I

Published some eighty years ago, George Dangerfield's *The Strange Death of Liberal England* remains a compelling and pertinent read. The nub of Dangerfield's thesis is that, contrary to the received wisdom of the times, the war of 1914–1918 was not to blame for the breakdown of Victorian liberalism; rather the decline of liberal England was the result of radical social forces that emerged in the early twentieth century. Additionally, whereas many of his middle-class contemporaries lamented the stability of high Victorianism (a cultural hegemony that lots of Edwardians took to be unassailable), Dangerfield cheerfully mocked the conventions and modes of conduct that were associated with a liberal parliamentary democracy, not least its civilised pretensions and political conservatism.

Nowadays, it would seem that we are witnessing the strange death of the liberal university. Various commentators have noted how British universities, though still non-profit charities, are being hastily fashioned after private companies.[1] The idea of the university as a place of civic education and critical enquiry has been hollowed out by a raft of neoliberal political rationalities that promote inter alia divisive competition, false economies, and philistine instrumentality. Academics are bound by ever multiplying forms of spurious measurement and performance management. Students, in turn, are treated more like consumers than they are citizens, increasingly defrauded with a candyfloss world of university branding and marketing gimmickry. Grant capture, consultancy, citations, impact, unique selling points, student surveys, and league tables have become the new deities that all shall worship.

Whilst the above developments have gathered apace since the financial crisis of 2007–2008, and the subsequent formation of broad-based campaign groups notwithstanding, recent criticisms of higher education marketisation have noted how UK academics are themselves partly to blame for the passing of academia as a liberal bastion: 'striking absence of powerful and united collective dissent', 'consensual silence', 'docile polity', 'almost complete capitulation', are just some of the charges that have been leveled at university lecturers and professors.[2] And those academics that do attempt to retain their integrity by refusing to observe the 'Gospel of Mammonism' risk being inculpated of error, blasphemy, heresy even. Censure, denunciation, and excommunication soon follow if the accused declines penance and reconciliation.

II

Not surprisingly, university scholars have long failed to defend intellectual liberty or to confront inconvenient home truths. Writing at the turn of the twentieth century, the Cambridge classicist-cum-satirist, F. M. Cornford, cautioned junior colleagues, especially the 'young men in a hurry' with a conscience, to heed the 'Principle of the dangerous precedent', which is to say:

> that you should not now do an admittedly right action for fear you, or your equally timid successors, should not have the courage to do right in some future case, which, ex hypothesi, is essentially different, but superficially resembles the present one. Every public action, which is not customary, either is wrong, or, if it is right, is a dangerous precedent. It follows that nothing should ever be done for the first time.[3]

Reflecting on his travels through the industrial heartlands of Yorkshire and Lancashire during the 'hungry thirties', George Orwell aimed much of his polemic, not at Westminster, but at the failings of self-styled metropolitan intellectuals who 'get on' by 'kissing the bums of verminous little lions', and whose left-wing opinions are 'mainly spurious'.[4] Elsewhere he famously likened the passivity of many of his liberal-Left contemporaries to the biblical story of Jonah:

> being inside a whale is a very comfortable, cosy, home-like thought. ... There you are, in the dark, cushioned space that exactly fits you, with yards of blubber between yourself and reality, able to keep up an attitude

of the completest indifference, no matter *what* happens. ... Short of being dead, it is the final, unsurpass-
able stage of irresponsibility.[5]

It was in a like fashion that Edward Thompson noted the reactionary and self-regarding nature of the species *Academicus
Superciliosus*, 'the most divisible and rulable creature in this
country', following the exposé of the so-called 'Warwick files'
controversy in the early 1970s.[6] Living their lives as if 'struck by
a paralysis of will' and 'in a kind of Awe of Propriety', Thompson opined that though talk of academic freedom 'is forever
on their lips', academics are in fact 'the last people to whom it
can be safely entrusted, since the present moment is never the
opportune moment to stand and fight.'[7] And just as Orwell was
concerned for the future of 'the autonomous individual' in the
face of totalitarianism, Thompson was equally troubled by the
emerging 'new methods of management', their 'insistence upon
the subjugation of the individual to institutional loyalties', and
'attempts to enforce loyalties by moral or disciplinary means, by
streaming procedures or by managing promotions and career
prospects.'[8] Finally, with his usual prophetic boldness, and with
Julien Benda's *La Trahison des clercs* in mind, Thompson predicted that most university teachers would retreat 'within the
limited area of manoeuvre allotted to him within the managerial structure.'[9]

More recently, former Essex professor and literary critic,
Marina Warner, has voiced several scathing criticisms about
her own unfortunate experience of university managerialism,
whilst simultaneously recognising that she herself may have
been 'naive, culpably unobservant as I went about my activities at Essex.'[10] Putting aside the personal circumstances that

caused her to quit Essex and the resulting commotion (which are widely known and do not need repeating here), much of what Warner has said hits its targets; moreover, her general observations throw further light on the sinister forces presently at play within British universities and their damaging effects: 'the culture of obedience and deference' that is cultivated through 'fear, insecurity, precarious social conditions and shame'; 'the silence of no comment which universities resort to when confronted with protests and complaints'; and if all else fails, constructive dismissal and the use of 'gagging orders'.[11] Warner's most damning indictment, however, is her likening of UK higher education and its 'rulers' ideas' to 'the world of Chinese communist corporatism':

> where enforcers rush to carry out the latest orders from their chiefs in an ecstasy of obedience to ideological principles which they do not seem to have examined, let alone discussed with the people they order to follow them, whom they cashier when they won't knuckle under.[12]

III

Not unlike the three wise monkeys who 'see no evil, hear no evil, speak no evil', rather than face down the conditions of their present existence, too many workers in UK universities have chosen to turn a blind eye or to actively collaborate, accommodating here, profiting there: the module leader who yields to pressures to raise his assessment marks because it will assist with bureaucratic rankings; the social scientist who is coerced into doctoring his research to make it more palatable to external funders and corporate sponsors; the ardent feminist who barely reacts when a fellow female colleague is hounded out of her job because she raised concerns about the predatory behavior of a male colleague; the faculty dean who champions privacy as an sacrosanct human right, yet cooperates with the security authorities to facilitate the surveillance of a 'politically difficult' colleague; the once radical Marxist who cares more about her professorial entitlements than she does workplace democracy; the duplicitous colleague who smears another colleague in an effort to curry favor and advance her career; the research development manager who regularly commits false accounting when costing university funding applications; the failed journalist who ends up working as a communications officer and is tasked with using her media contacts to censor academics who are not on message; the head of department who uses departmental funds to surreptitiously employ a personal researcher to write his four REF articles; the dishonourable member of senior management who wheels and deals in backhanders and embezzlement; the human resources officer who fabricates trumped-up charges to force somebody out of the institution; above all, the ever more characteristic vice chancellor whose sole ambition is to climb the establishment's greasy pole (that peculiarly English system of patronage otherwise known as 'Old Corruption'), and who readily abuses his office by victimising dissenting voices whilst simulating a cynical facade of Arnoldian sweetness and light.

These are just some of the distortions and hidden injuries of the UK higher education sector. And though some of the above wrongdoings can be put down to everyday careerism, hypocrisy, and cowardice, others are symptomatic of an increasingly marketised system that encourages and rewards unfettered commercialism, bullying, and deceit.

Such developments are furthered by a new cadre of university managers who have become a class apart, an oligarchical elite who have allowed the big battalions of capital to mass their tanks on academia's borders. It is for these reasons that Thomas Docherty has argued that 'we are perilously close to a position where the unquestioned power of management is declaring war on the academic community, the university, itself: civil war in academia.'[13] Faced with such a situation, academics, administrators, and students have a choice. We can continue to acquiesce to the whimsical demands of politicians and their stooges in the pessimistic belief that there is no alternative. Or, and to return to George Dangerfield and the decline of parliamentary liberalism in early twentieth-century Britain, colleagues *could* choose to bear witness to everything that is happening in academia, warts and all, and thus bid farewell to that 'fine old Liberal Hegelianism of at once believing in freedom and not believing in freedom'. Anything less risks universities being turned into enemies of democratic criticism and intellectual honesty; in fact, it would be tantamount to the strange death of the liberal university by assisted suicide.

Notes

1. For example, Michael Bailey and Des Freedman eds., *The Assault on Universities: A Manifesto for Resistance* (London: Pluto Press, 2011); Roger Brown and Helen Carasso, *Everything for Sale? The Marketization of UK Higher Education* (London: Routledge and the Society for Research into Higher Education, 2013); Stefan Collini, *What Are Universities For?* (Harmondsworth, UK: Penguin, 2012); Thomas Docherty, *Universities at War* (London: SAGE Swifts, 2014); John Holmwood, ed., *A Manifesto for the Public University*

(London: Bloomsbury, 2011); Andrew McGettigan, *The Great University Gamble: Money, Markets and the Future of Higher Education* (London: Pluto Press, 2013).

2. Priyamvada Gopal, "Viewpoint: The Assault on Higher Education and Democracy," *Discover Society* 5, (February 15, 2014), http://discoversociety
.org/2014/02/15/viewpoint-the-assault-on-higher-education-and-democracy;
Jon Nixon, *Higher Education and the Public Good: Imagining the University* (London: Continuum, 2011), 6; Fred Inglis, "Today's Intellectuals: Too Obedient?," *Times Higher Education* (August 28, 2014); "Interview: Terry Eagleton," by John Schad, *Times Higher Education*, January 8, 2015, https://www
.timeshighereducation.com/features/interview-terry-eagleton/2017733.article.

3. F. M. Cornford, *Microcosmographia Academica: Being A Guide for the Young Academic Politician* (Cambridge: Metcalfe, 1908), 15.

4. George Orwell, *The Road to Wigan Pier* (Harmondsworth, UK: Penguin, 1989), 152–53.

5. George Orwell, *Inside the Whale and Other Essays* (Harmondsworth, UK: Penguin, 1984), 42–43.

6. E. P. Thompson ed., *Warwick University Ltd.: Industry, Management and the Universities* (Harmondsworth, UK: Penguin, 1970), 53.

7. Ibid., 154–55.

8. Ibid., 162–63.

9. Ibid., 163–64.

10. Marina Warner, "Learning My Lesson," *London Review of Books* 37, no. 6 (2015), 8–14.

11. Ibid.; see also, Marina Warner, "Attempts to 'Gag and Silence' Academics Are Commonplace," *Times Higher Education* (September 11, 2014).

12. Marina Warner, "Diary," *London Review of Books* 36, no. 17 (September 11, 2014), 42–43.

13. Thomas Docherty, "On Academic Freedom," *Times Higher Education* (December 4, 2014).

32

A Dialogue between Enlightenment Liberals and Neoliberal Elites on the Idea of the University

Joan Pedro-Carañana

Based upon a real story ...

Society pays to make the education system a crock of shit because the dumber the people are that come out, the easier it is to draft them, make them into docile consumers, or, you know, mongo employees. There are plenty of yuppies out there with absolutely nothing upstairs. Graduate airheads with PhDs and everything but they don't know anything.
—Attributed to Frank Zappa

From the quest for truth to the search for obedience and do-cility, the depictions of higher education vary according to the priorities underlying your particular idea of the university. What follows is an exercise in sociological imagination in which those leading the reform of universities in Europe today enter into a dialogue with Enlightenment thinkers of education. This fictional conversation is based on the actual words and ideas of the respective actors and takes place in the context of the current ambitious plans for the advancement of a European Higher Education Area (EHEA).

On the right side of the stage are the European Ministers of Education,[1] who signed the Bologna Declaration that has driven the process of globalisation and convergence of higher education, and that was followed by a large number of declarations and programs that have been established by both European institutions and national governments. Opposite to the ministers are Enlightenment figures who presented ideas that forwarded the emergence of the first liberal universities at the end of the eighteenth and beginning of the nineteenth centuries, including Kant, Humboldt, Godwin, Reynolds, and Rousseau.

The beginning of the conversation dates back to 1988, when the rectors of European universities meet in Bologna to sign the *Magna Charta Universitatum* and note the upcoming internationalisation and transformation of societies. As experienced academics in this dialogue, the rectors get in touch with Kant and Humboldt and agree to include the notion that the university is expected to promote cultural, scientific, and technical knowledge, upon which depends 'the future of mankind.'[2] They concur that the dissemination of knowledge to both new generations and to the whole of society will ensure the cultural, social, and economic future of society.

All are in agreement, but Humboldt insists on mentioning the principle forwarded by the Scientific Revolution of 'harmonious' and 'active' relations between humans and nature as allies belonging to the same unity.[3] The rectors note that some conflicts between humans and nature may arise and write in the *Magna Charta* that the university must 'respect the great harmonies of their natural environment and life.'[4]

For universities to achieve their missions, the *Magna Charta* takes up Enlightenment principles that surely sound appealing: academic freedom and institutional autonomy guaranteed by universities and public authorities vis-à-vis any political, economic, or ideological force; the unity of teaching and research; dialogue between teachers and students; and reciprocal knowledge and interaction of the tradition of European humanism with other cultures beyond the continental borders.

Ten years later, the Ministers of Education of France, Germany, Italy and the United Kingdom sign the *Declaration of the Sorbonne*,[5] which introduces important changes in the project of creating a European space devoted to higher education. Humboldt feels anxious about a new element that was not present in the *Magna Charta*: there is an excess of emphasis on the professional dimension of knowledge that supposedly prepares the graduates to be better adapted to the labour market. Humboldt replies that 'he is only a good worker or business seller who is, by himself and without regard to his specific job, a kind, decent and enlightened man and citizen, according to his possibilities.' Education should focus on the intellectual and human dimensions so that graduates 'will learn later the specific skills of their trade with ease and keep the freedom, as often happens in life, to change professions.'[6] Rousseau weighs in: 'In the natural order of things, all men being equal, their common vocation is manhood. ... To live is the trade I wish to teach. ... Whoever is well trained for that cannot fulfil badly any vocation connected with it.'[7]

The European Ministers of Education choose to ignore the complaints and in the *Bologna Declaration* of 1999[8] confirm their adherence to the ideas agreed in the *Sorbonne* statement, reaffirming their commitment to promoting the convergence of university systems. The Enlightenment thinkers analyse the *Declaration,* as well as some drafts of the working documents of the EHEA that have been leaked. They highlight the proposal of adapting the university to technological innovation and the development of a so-called knowledge-based economy, which can be globally competitive, enable the modernisation of enterprises, boost economic growth and, ideally, create more and better jobs. Joshua Reynolds stresses that he understands that the ministers may be well-meaning, but that this reform gets wrong the means and the ends: 'Commerce is the means, not the end of happiness or pleasure: the end is a rational enjoyment of life, by the means of arts and sciences.'[9]

The European authorities complain about the leak and point out that they have to learn from the past if they want to win the debate and develop their EHEA. Remember what happened in France with the Enlightenment? The Revolution disrupted the social order and put an end to the established authorities. Control was lost amidst the disarray, until Napoleon reasserted bourgeois hegemony along despotic and modernising lines, centralising the university system to place it at the service of the imperial state. Auguste Comte bequeathed to the future leaders the idea that publicists can make use of social scientific tools to persuade the majority that the negative effects of capitalist development are merely unavoidable costs of progress. In order to turn positivist-technocratic university and social reforms into a desirable prospect, it would be necessary to incorporate strategies, written in Orwellian language, for domestic and international consumption.

European leaders feel ready now to hold a new meeting with their adversaries of the past. They explain that the drafts were not complete and that they have developed the social aspects of their proposal. They decide to foreground the idea that the university should contribute to the improvement of social cohesion, equality of opportunity, respect for human rights, and protection of the environment by fostering learn-ing, research, and innovation that would contribute to 'the development and strengthening of stable, peaceful and dem-ocratic societies'.[10]

Some Enlightenment thinkers feel satisfied, while others, such as William Godwin, remain sceptical. He calls a meeting to organize the resistance where he quotes a passage he had written in 1793, adapting it by adding an international perspective and labelling it *Bologna Rewinds*: 'The project of a national educa-tion ought uniformly to be discouraged on account of its obvious alliance with national government. This is an alliance of a more formidable nature, than the old and much contested alliance of church and state. Before we put so powerful a machine under the direction of so ambiguous an agent, it behoves us to consider well what it is that we do. Government will not fail to employ it to strengthen its hands, and perpetuate its institutions.'[11]

Conversations continue and the European leaders argue that there is no alternative to the Bologna process: competitive universities are needed to ensure the competitiveness of Eu-rope in a global age.[12]

Humboldt explains that cooperation and not competition is the fundamental principle for the advancement of knowledge and humanity. However, the ministers had anticipated the criti-cism and reply that obviously they have also included guide-lines about the cooperation needed for the success of the EHEA. Enlightenment thinkers remain unconvinced and condemn the excessive emphasis on business and market criteria such as efficiency and profit making. They focus on the funding mecha-nisms, noting that the European Commission warned already in 2003, that 'the growing shortfall' in funding means that 'ways have to be found of increasing and diversifying universities' income.'[13] Marketing for fundraising becomes central. Private investment must be encouraged on par with the principles of public responsibility and autonomy of universities.[14]

Enlightened opposition to the marketisation of universities leads to divisions among ministers. In the Bucharest meeting of 2012, a real-life, non-fictional debate takes place between supporters of making a commitment to ensuring public funding and those opposing them.[15] The final version of the *Declaration*, notes that 'the crisis is affecting the availability of adequate funding' and commits to 'securing the highest possible level of public funding for higher education and drawing on other appropriate sources, as an investment in our future.'[16]

This turn in funding strategies generates important controversies. Enlightenment thinkers wonder if it is compatible with equality, permanent learning, and the university autonomy the reform proposes to strengthen. The authorities argue that 'universities' independence and autonomy ensure that higher education and research systems continuously adapt to [the] changing needs' of society, for example, by adapting the syllabus to the needs of the job market as established in Bologna.[17] Humboldt answers by explaining the Enlightenment principles of combining the teaching and research of science with the pedagogical stance to promote the fullest development of each citizen, according to his or her own capacities and interests, with the aim of advancing the culture that orients the human impulses towards curious inquiry and creative work. He notes that these principles are inverted and perverted when education is instrumentalised for extraneous purposes such as the needs of economic institutions. Autonomy *within* the framework of the market or any other external power is not autonomy *from* the system. The university will not be able to fulfil its mission of searching for truth for the development of humanity (i.e., 'to give the fullest possible content to the concept of humanity in our own person ... through the impact of actions in our own lives').[18] The response was to be expected and was on the following lines:

> Dear Humboldt, your view belongs to the past; it is time for universities to abandon the ivory tower. For example, it is essential to furnish a Digital Agenda, so that continuous learning and research adapt to the necessities of the economy and increasingly provide training for specialised personnel in ICTs and electronic businesses.[19]

Kant laments that the authorities of the twenty-first century treat the works of the Enlightenment as relics, while not seeming to have actually read them. He points out what he had already written more than two centuries ago: 'Children ought to be educated, not for the present, but for a possibly improved condition of man in the future; that is, in a manner which is adapted to the *idea of humanity* and the whole destiny of man.'[20]

At this point the conversation reaches a stalemate. Enlightenment personalities argue that modern administrations are not able to understand their humanist dialogue. To finish their meeting, they note that it is up to the twenty-first-century generations to advance the endless process of humanisation of societies by reaffirming university autonomy, cooperation, equality, rational analysis, harmony with nature, and passionate freedom. These are Enlightenment principles that have been compromised by the ongoing adjustment of knowledge and human beings to a technocratic, global market.

Notes

1. Ministers of Education of France, Germany, Italy, and the United Kingdom, "Sorbonne Joint Declaration," Paris, the Sorbonne, May 25, 1998, accessed February 20, 2016, http://media.ehea.info/file/1998_Sorbonne/61/2/1998_Sorbonne_Declaration_English_552612.pdf.

2. Rectors, "Magna Charta Universitatum," Bologna, September 18, 1988, accessed February 20, 2016, http://www.magna-charta.org/resources/files/the-magna-charta/english.

3. Quoted in Gerd Hohendorf, "Wilhelm von Humboldt: 1767–1835," *Prospects* 23, no. 3/4 (1993): 613–23. doi:10.1007/BF02195142.

4. Rectors, *Magna Charta.*

5. Ministers, "Sorbonne Joint Declaration."

6. Quoted in Antonio Aguilera-Fernández, "La Prevaricación del Buen Lenguaje y de la Libertad y Derecho Constitucional," *Nómadas. Revista Crítica de Ciencias Sociales y Jurídicas* 31, no. 3 (2011): 225–36.

7. Jean-Jacques Rousseau, *Rousseau's Émile; or Treatise on Education* (New York: D. Appleton, 1918), 8.

8. European Ministers of Education, "The Bologna Declaration," June 19, 1999, accessed February 20, 2016, http://media.ehea.info/file/Ministerial_conferences/02/8/1999_Bologna_Declaration_English_553028.pdf.

9. Quoted in John Brewer, *The Pleasures of the Imagination: English Culture in the Eighteenth Century* (Abingdon, UK: Routledge, 2013), 294.

10. Ministers, "The Bologna Declaration."

11. William Godwin, *An Enquiry Concerning Political Justice*, vol. 2, (Charlottesville, VA: Electronic Text Center, University of Virginia Library, [1793]), bk. 6, chap. 8, http://oll.libertyfund.org/titles/236.

12. See Council of the European Union, "Resolution on Modernising Universities for Europe's Competitiveness in a Global Knowledge Economy," Brussels, November 23, 2007, accessed February 20, 2016, http://www.consilium.europa.eu/uedocs/cms_Data/docs/pressdata/en/intm/97237.pdf; European Commission, "Horizon 2020 – The Framework Programme for Research and Innovation," Brussels, November 30, 2011, accessed February 20, 2016, http://eur-lex.europa.eu/legal-content/EN/TXT/PDF/?uri=CELEX:5201 1DC0808&from=EN.

13. European Commission, "The Role of Universities in the Europe of Knowledge," (February 5, 2003), accessed February 20, 2016, http://eur-lex.europa.eu/LexUriServ/LexUriServ.do?uri=COM:2003:0058:FIN:EN:PDF, 12.

14. European Ministers of Education, "London Communiqué: Towards the European Higher Education Area: Responding to Challenges in a Globalised World," May 18, 2007, accessed February 20, 2016, https://www.eqar.eu/fileadmin/documents/bologna/London-Communique-18May2007.pdf; "The Bologna Process 2020—The European Higher Education Area in the New Decade: Communiqué of the Conference of European Ministers Responsible for Higher Education," April, 2009, accessed February 20, 2016, http://www.ond.vlaanderen.be/hogeronderwijs/bologna/conference/documents/leuven_louvain-la-neuve_communiqu%C3%A9_april_2009.pdf.

15. FE-CCOO, "La Declaración de Bucarest o el Último Asalto Privatizador al Proceso de Bolonia. Una Crónica," May 8, 2012, accessed February 20, 2016, http://feccoocant-universidad.blogspot.com.es/2012/05/la-declaracion-de-bucarest-o-el-ultimo.html.

16. European Ministers of Education, "Mobility for Better Learning. Mobility Strategy 2020 for the European Higher Education Area (EHEA)," Bucharest, 2012, accessed February 20, 2016, http://media.ehea.info/file/2012_Bucharest/39/2/2012_EHEA_Mobility_Strategy_606392.pdf.

17. European Ministers of Education, "The Bologna Declaration," June 19, 1999, accessed February 20, 2016, http://media.ehea.info/file/Ministerial_conferences/02/8/1999_Bologna_Declaration_English_553028.pdf.

18. Quoted in Hohendorf, "Wilhelm von Humboldt," 622.

19. European Commission, "Digital Agenda for Europe," last modified June 25, 2010, accessed February 20, 2016, http://europa.eu/legislation_summaries/information_society/strategies/si0016_en.htm.

20. Immanuel Kant, *On Education* (Mineola, NY: Dover, 2012), 14.

IV

Liberalism, Race, and Gender

The much-celebrated 1789 'Declaration of the Rights of Man and of the Citizen'—a foundational Enlightenment document—did indeed define the individual and collective rights of all the estates of the realm as universal. The rights were qualified as 'natural, unalienable and sacred', and the first article proudly announced that 'men are born and remain free and equal in rights. Social distinctions may be founded only upon the general good.' Yet the declaration neither revoked slavery nor recognised the equal rights of women. Why were the calls and petitions for recognising equal rights not applied to all people? Was this a simple accident or omission? How compatible is the universalism of liberal ideology with the system of hierarchies that is preserved and maintained in contemporary capitalist societies? To what extent are racism and sexism anomalies or part of the very system that has been shaped and defined by the very paradox of its own universality?

Favourable accounts of liberalism often fail to mention those exclusion clauses that play a significant role in its history.

Liberty, in its broader sense, needs to be linked to the question of equality and to the conditions that make it possible for freedom and equality to be absent or present. For Étienne Balibar, this means that 'the diverse forms of social and political "power" that correspond to either inequalities or constraints on the freedom of man the citizen necessarily converge. There are no examples of restrictions or suppressions neither of freedoms without social inequalities, nor of inequalities without restrictions or suppressions of freedoms.'[1] This section, therefore, engages with the limits, contradictions, and exclusive clauses in liberal thought and practice as applied to issues of race and gender.

Note

1. Étienne Balibar, *Masses, Classes, Ideas: Studies on Politics and Philosophy Before and After Marx* (New York: Routledge, 1994), 49.

33

Liberalism and Gender

Milly Williamson

The issue of gender freedom is one that is often raised when favourably contrasting liberal Western societies with other (in particular today, Muslim) parts of the world. The idea of freedom is fundamental to liberalism's claims to legitimacy and ideological hegemony. Female emancipation is seen as a great triumph of liberal thought and action—women in Western liberal democracies are enfranchised, and are seen to have formal equality under the law in the areas of employment, pay, and in control over their bodies. Women's emancipation is seen as central to an understanding of modernity, it is seen as a marker of a progressive society, and as such contributes to liberalism's sense of pre-eminence.

There are, however, considerable problems with this picture, which obscures the reality of the limits of liberalism. Liberal thought and practice makes claims to universal human value while historically excluding large sections of the population from democratic rights and freedoms—including women, the working class, the enslaved populations of Africa, and the populations of European colonies. These significant limits of liberal democracy stem from the historical conditions that gave rise to it; mass revolution followed quickly by reaction in the late eighteenth and then again in the nineteenth century resulted in the domination of a single class who, as Marx argued, established constitutional democracies on the principle of freedom, but who limited those principles from the outset through legal curtailments.[1] Liberal democracy presented itself as a universal system when in fact, constitutional democracies were shaped by the class interests of an economic elite.

Women were legally excluded from the gains of this new democratic order and these exclusions were supported ideologically by prominent liberal philosophers such as Jean-Jacques Rousseau and Charles Maurice de Talleyrand-Périgord who argued that women were naturally inferior to men and declared that women did not need an education, other than that which pleases man. Mary Wollstonecraft published the *Vindication of the Rights of Woman* in 1792[2]—the first manifesto of female emancipation—as a refutation of these views on women, and she particularly attacked Jean-Jacques Rousseau, whose traditional views on female inferiority were considered by Wollstonecraft to be a painful betrayal of liberalism. But these traditional ideas (that women are inferior to men and should be kept in a state of dependency) are not a betrayal of liberalism—instead, they were at the heart of liberal thinking, which, in the nineteenth century revived classical ideas about biological divisions between populations, 'races', and gender in order to justify the Atlantic slave trade, European imperialism, and female subordination.

It was not until the 1970s that women were granted legal equality on the question of work, pay, and education, and these were not bestowed by liberal regimes, but were a product of struggles against them. Prior to 1970 women did not have the right to demand equal pay under the law and it was perfectly legal to discriminate against women at work, while advances such as the Equal Pay Act of 1970 was the direct result of a strike by female car factory workers in Dagenham, rather than benign liberal intervention. As Domenico Losurdo argues, at its height there were three 'macroscopic exclusions' in liberal notions of freedom—the oppressed colonial subject and the enslaved African, the exploited worker in the metropolitan centers, and women.[3] Losurdo makes a strong case that the freedom of the liberal, property-owning classes in the West actually depended on these exclusions, and one can argue that liberal regimes today continue to depend on the exclusion of subaltern groups from full political participation, as election turnouts in the United Kingdom have steadily declined since 1950.[4]

Nonetheless, one of liberalism's greatly proclaimed achievements is universal suffrage, including women's suffrage. On this count too, however, liberalism had to be forced to concede the vote in response to mass dissent. In the United Kingdom, many suffragettes were imprisoned and violently force-fed while on hunger strike. The vote was only conceded to women in Britain in 1928. In some liberal democracies full female suffrage came even later—France in 1945, Italy in 1946, Switzerland in 1972, and Liechtenstein in 1984! The advances in gender equality have been made by challenges to such liberal democracies rather than as an outcome of liberal philosophy or deliberation—liberal thought was forced to adopt the principles of democracy—and at great cost. Overcoming the exclusion of women from the liberal sphere of political equality, just as an end to the slave trade and of European empires, was the outcome, not of liberal reform, but of violent upheavals. The realisation of women's political rights was the consequence of struggle that had the violence of the First World War behind it and the revolutionary upheavals of the early twentieth century in front.

And, as in the cases of class and race, complete gender equality and emancipation have not yet been fully achieved in the liberal West (over a century and a half after the bourgeois revolutions that swept away the old order and swept in modern liberal democracies). Full voting rights have not produced female emancipation. Liberal thinking, in equating political freedom with economic or social freedom, disavows the inequality and unfreedom that arises from a lack of social justice. Indeed, the liberal wing of the feminist movement in the nineteenth and early twentieth century, by adhering to the liberal tenets on the separation of political rights and economic rights, and focussing almost exclusively on the franchise, not only made an appalling historic compromise in supporting the First World War with the promise of the vote, but also wrongly believed that when the vote was obtained, the struggle for equal rights would be won. This divided the struggle for female suffrage from other feminist struggles, and from those in the socialist movement advocating a challenge to the basic social structure and calling for economic and social justice as well as political rights. Almost a century since women won the vote, women still only make up 22 per cent of MPs—a total of 143 out of 650. More than four decades after equal pay was enshrined in law (1970) women still earn two-thirds of male earnings, and more than three decades after equal rights legislation on work (1975), discrimination at work is rampant, and women are still predominantly employed in the low-paid service sector and social services. And it is women, particularly working-class women and women of colour, who are bearing the brunt of austerity measures, (including the attacks on welfare, depressed wages, and the rising cost of living), that are designed to cut the size of the national debt following the bailout of banks; the same banks whose 'freedom' from regulation precipitated the financial crash in 2008. Liberalism's promise of freedom and equality was never intended for the majority, but for the propertied elite, and the advances made by women, workers, and the anti-racist movement have been under sustained attack from our liberal rulers almost from the moment they were won.

And yet important sections of liberal feminism have, in this context, not allied themselves to those who wish to see a redistribution of wealth and a defence of welfare, but instead is attacking them. Prominent feminists such as darling of the right-wing press, Jess Phillips, have recently accused the UK socialist leader of the opposition, Jeremy Corbyn, of misogyny, despite his record on supporting feminism, women's strikes, and the fact that his shadow cabinet is made up of 50 per cent women, for the first time in the history of British politics. Phillips accuses Corbyn of keeping the 'top jobs' for men and reprimands female supporters of the Corbyn campaign for their 'complicity'.[5] (This is despite female MPs appointed as shadow Secretary of State, the Treasury, Climate Change, Chief Whip, Education, Defence, the Environment, Transport, etc.) Harriet Harman repeated the message about a male dominated shadow cabinet, despite fifteen out of thirty shadow cabinet positions going to women, and both she and Phillips have been widely reported with glee across the right-wing media in the United Kingdom.[6]

Phillips' claims that left-wing Labour feminists are putting up with misogyny from Corbyn is simply dressing up an attack on the Left in pseudo-feminist language from the centre-right who do not wish to see the Blairite New Labour project removed from centre stage of the Labour Party. Let us not forget the political and gender make-up of Blair's cabinets, or the women who were reshuffled out on a regular basis (including Harriet Harman, who like Blair himself did not support women shortlists, and did not speak out against the demeaning phrase 'Blair's Babes' attached to women MPs after the 1997 landslide Labour victory).

The pattern of leading female politicians using feminism to attack feminists who support left-wing politics has also occurred in the US race for presidential nominations. While socialist Democratic nominee and political outsider, Bernie Sanders, has managed to secure overwhelming support amongst young feminists who see Hillary Clinton as representative of a political establishment they loathe,[7] Clinton herself has 'aggressively reached out to young women' unsuccessfully while her supporter Madeleine Albright claimed 'there was a special place in hell' for women who did not vote for Clinton.[8] These attacks, just like those in the United Kingdom, are using the language of feminism (or at least a liberal version) in order to try to discredit socialist politics—the historic challenger to liberal philosophy and the practices of liberal regimes—with its offer of an alternative political vision that demands not just political equality, but also economic justice, and social equality.

Notes

1. Karl Marx, *The Eighteenth Brumaire of Louis Bonaparte*. (New York: Cosimo Classics, 2008); Karl Marx, *Grundrisse*, trans. Martin Nicolous (London: Penguin, 1993).
2. Mary Wollstonecraft, *Vindication of the Rights of Woman* (London: Penguin, 2004).

3. Domenico Losurdo, *Liberalism: A Counter-History*, trans. Gregory Elliott (London: Verso, 2011), 181.

4. "General Election Turnout 1945–2015," *UK Political Info*, accessed March 11, 2016, http://www.ukpolitical.info/Turnout45.htm.

5. Ned Simons, "Labour Feminists Letting Jeremy Corbyn Get Away with Misogyny, Says Jess Phillips," *Huffington Post*, January 5, 2016, UK edition, accessed March 11, 2016, http://www.huffingtonpost.co.uk/2016/01/05/labour-feminists-letting-corbyn-get-away-with-misogyny-says-mp_n_8914972.html.

6. Jenny Parks, "Harriet Harman: Labour Needs Ban on All-Male Leadership," *BBC News*, January 4, 2016, accessed March 11, 2016, http://www.bbc.co.uk/news/uk-politics-35225175.

7. Evan Halper, "Why Young Feminists Are Choosing Bernie Sanders over Hillary Clinton," *Los Angeles Times*, February 4, 2016, accessed March 11, 2016, http://www.latimes.com/politics/la-na-clinton-millennial-women-20160203-story.html.

8. Tom McCarthy, "Albright: 'Special Place in Hell' for Women Who Don't Support Clinton," *Guardian*, February 6, 2016, accessed March 11, 2016, http://www.theguardian.com/us-news/2016/feb/06/madeleine-albright-campaigns-for-hillary-clinton.

34

Zionism and Liberalism: Complementary or Contradictory?

Haim Bresheeth

Like many other national movements of the late nineteenth century, political Zionism was originally presented as part of the European liberal tradition, which reaches an important pitch in 1848. Mainly developed into a vibrant political movement by the author and journalist Theodor Herzl, a somewhat typical product of the Viennese Jewish bourgeoisie of the *fin de siècle*, Herzl was also a typical right-wing liberal of his period; it is of course the period that sees general male suffrage in some countries (though not that of women), a large number of new nation states being established in Europe, and also the promising heights of modernism—a crucial trend in the arts, theatre, literature, architecture, and also early cinema—the iconic art form of modernity. This growing democratisation of the European polis is the fruit of the liberal development of a couple of centuries, at least. The apparent lessening of traditional anti-Semitism and the gradual endowing of Jews with human rights, has also been paralleled by the growth of new forms of anti-Semitism, supposedly scientific and using such approaches as phrenology to develop new Judophobia for the modern age; such were the attempts of the Action Française in France, for example, or the politics of the anti-Semitic Karl Lueger, who became mayor of Vienna just as Herzl was about to publish *Judenstaat*—his seminal Zionist text—in 1896. Arguably, the ascent of Lueger has hastened his conversion to Zionism, and his sense of urgency in offering a practical solution to the so-called "Jewish Question" in Europe.

Typically, European liberals such as Gladstone supported limited freeing-up of colonial societies, like in the case of the debate about Irish Home Rule during the 1880s, but never opposed new colonial ventures by Britain, such as the occupation of Egypt in 1882. The focus of such liberals was on free trade, laissez-faire economics, minimal government intervention, and individual freedoms, meaning freedoms for the middle classes. Of course, the *individual* was European by definition, and most of humanity, living elsewhere and in many cases under the control of European powers, were widely considered as natives and thus inferior, hence not eligible for the same rights as *individuals* in the so-called civilised nations.

This disturbing portfolio of policies suited Herzl perfectly, of course. His Zionism was presented as a project of freeing the Jews of Europe from centuries of racism by removing them to their ancestral home, whereby they will build a liberal European society in the midst of 'Asiatic despotism' and serve as the modern, European imperialist wedge in the backwards Arab and Muslim Middle East. As part of taking over Palestine, Herzl secretly describes (in his *Complete Diaries*)[1] the process of emptying the country of its 'paupers', meaning most of the indigenous population, in order to create a proper Jewish state—one with a decisive Jewish majority. This portion of his *Diaries* was systematically edited out of all earlier publications in either German, Hebrew, or English, and only came to be released in 1960. Hence he kept his 'liberal' veneer for decades after his death.

One needs to put this in historical perspective; when Herzl writes this, Jews in Palestine are about 8.5 per cent of the population, at 25,000. His plan to rid the country of more than 250,000 of its inhabitants was indeed audacious and even odious, but one has to remember that fifty years later this wish will come to pass.

This illiberal blueprint of early Zionism, hardly ever discussed in public, has been the mainstay of political Zionist thought and action ever since Herzl's death, and implemented in 1948, when the newly created Israel Defense Forces (IDF) has ethnically-cleansed four-fifths of Palestine of around 750,000 Palestinian inhabitants, or two-thirds of all Palestinian Arabs. In this whole period, only the brief episode of Brit Shalom, a left-leaning group of German liberals based in Jerusalem, advocating a binational state and open, equal relationship with the Arabs of Palestine, has offered anything but subjugation to the local population. Alas, they never accounted for more than a hundred people, and had no effect whatsoever on Zionist policies.

On the face of it, Herzl's political liberalism has affected Zionism even after his death. However, this is somewhat inaccurate when one considers the history of Zionism in detail. It was indeed in 1905, a short time after Herzl's death, that the future route of Zionism was changed dramatically, by the arrival of a few hundred Jewish socialists from Russia, after the failure of the 1905 Russian Revolution. This group, which was to be greatly strengthened over the next two decades, would become the dominant force of Palestine Zionism, pushing the Herzlian liberal Zionism into a historical corner, which it only escaped after 1977, when the first Begin government took power. The interregnum of seven decades would give birth to some innovative social formations, such as the Kibbutz, which were crucial for the capturing and controlling of Palestinian land and expanding the land-base of Zionism, as well as to its military expansion. In this long and troubled period, Zionism has abandoned its liberal roots, preferring instead a left-wing rhetoric of the industrial and agricultural working class, but clearly excluding any opportunity of rapprochement with the indigenous population, and acting as the core of a *Herrenvolk* democracy—a democracy for Jews only, excluding any option of *rapprochement* or co-existence with the indigenous population. On achieving statehood in 1948, Israel embarked on an anti-liberal agenda—an omnipotent, militaristic state, instigating mass ethnic cleansing, and placing the Palestinians left within its enlarged area under oppressive military government that lasted until 1964, when the statist (a practitioner of the French politics of étatisme) Ben-Gurion left the political scene. During this period, the Histadruth, the federation of trade unions, owned and controlled up to two-thirds of all production, export and import, and was the largest employer in the country. The liberal Zionist project seemed at an end, and some naive European socialists mistook this militaristic colonial state for a socialist polity, unaware of the background described. The Kibbutz gap-year became de rigueur for young European lefties.

The political upheaval of 1977, when the castigated Israeli liberal Right captured power from the collectivist Left, has seemingly changed Zionism for ever. Even when governments of the 'Left' were in power since 1977, the (neo)liberal social politics of laissez-faire, mass privatisation of socialised resources and services, and support of deep inequalities has not been rescinded. Post 1977, the massive social structures of left-wing Zionism were quickly and efficiently taken apart, the union movement decimated, and the Kibbutzim that helped to steal so much of Palestine's land became some of the richest landowners in Israel, employers of *Gastarbeiter* from across the globe, on punitive and inhuman contracts. Israeli capitalism, under this new social regime, became the strongest in the Middle East, controlling massive empires of media, building, armaments, and hi-tech industries. Israel's neoliberal economy is one of the strongest in the world, based on the captive market of six million Palestinians, two-thirds being stateless and lacking any human or employment rights, and the insatiable global thirst for arms and new technologies; it is also supported by huge capital transfers from the United States—making up more than half of all US aid globally. The longish episode of left-wing, racist, and militarist étatisme, has been replaced by a no less militaristic, neoliberal, racist apartheid state, which, while professing neoliberal values, is continuing the illegal occupation, barbaric war crimes in Gaza and elsewhere, and the denial of rights to millions, as well as squeezing its own citizens, serving the narrow financial elite ruling the country.

All of which never stopped Israeli propaganda using liberal intellectuals as the mainstay of its work abroad, of course. Audiences in many countries are aware of the famous trio of authors—David Grossman, A. B. Yehoshua, and Amos Oz, who are the permanent whitewashers of Israeli policies, travelling around the globe financed by various Israeli Ministries—as evidence of the open-minded Israeli society—allowed their mild critical edge as proof of Israeli liberality. Israel has realised sometime ago that it is better defended by mild critics, than by fervent ideologues. The current extreme government seems to have forgotten this lesson.

The attack on Gaza in summer 2014 is a case in point. Throughout the murderous onslaught on a large civilian, helpless conurbation, Israeli propaganda used the mantras 'Israel has a right to defend itself' and 'thousands of rockets are raining over Israel'. These were uttered not only by the IDF spokespersons, but also by the seasoned liberals, whose voice carries more weight abroad. Listening to them, one could imagine that Israel was under the Blitz, and had no choice but to react and defend itself. The realities were different, of course—the 'thousands of rockets' harmed some six people in Israel, (66 soldiers were killed in fighting with resistance fighters inside Gaza) while the bombing of Gaza, in 51 days, amounted to *twice* the weight of high explosives dumped on London during the Blitz, killing over 2,200 people, injuring over 13,000, making 110,000 people homeless, and destroying most of Gaza's infrastructure, not for the first time. In the best liberal traditions of disregarding the humanity of indigenous populations, the trio of liberal literary musketeers and their allies in academia and the arts, found it acceptable to defend the war crimes of Israel's government. It must be a unique object lesson in how the term *liberal* may be stretched to a breaking point.

Note

1. Theodor Herzl, *The Complete Diaries of Theodor Herzl,* trans. Harry Zohn, ed. Raphael Patai (London: Herzl Press and Thomas Yoseloff, 1960), 88.

35

Ending Racial Oppression Means Transcending the Limits of Liberal Politics

Arun Kundnani

On the October 3, 2014 edition of his *Real Time* show on HBO, host Bill Maher told his audience: 'Liberals need to stand up for liberal principles' and that 'in the Muslim world, this is what's lacking'. His guest, atheist writer Sam Harris, went on to state that 'Islam is the mother lode of bad ideas' and that 'we are misled to think the fundamentalists are the fringe'. Actor Ben Affleck responded by telling Maher and Harris he found their views 'gross and racist', prompting the segment to go viral.

The exchange prompted much discussion on whether Harris and Maher's comments are factually accurate descriptions of Muslim belief or crude generalisations. Of course, in many Muslim-majority countries, there are ongoing political struggles for gender equality, freedom of expression, freedom of religion, and LGBT rights, which any liberal or Leftist ought to support. But such struggles are not unique to Muslim-majority countries. Maher and Harris allege that human rights problems in what they reductively call 'the Muslim world' are caused by

Islam, as if it is a monolith that mechanically drives people who believe in it to acts of barbarism.

But beliefs reflect social conditions as much as they shape them. Polls of global public opinion suggest that whether one thinks, for example, that violence against civilians is legitimate has more to do with political context than religious belief; and such violence is considered more acceptable in the United States and Europe than everywhere else in the world.[1]

Indeed, Sam Harris himself has written in support of killing civilians for the beliefs they hold. In his book *The End of Faith*, he says: 'Some propositions are so dangerous that it may even be ethical to kill people for believing them. ... This is what the United States attempted in Afghanistan, and it is what we and other Western powers are bound to attempt, at an even greater cost to ourselves and to innocents abroad, elsewhere in the Muslim world. We will continue to spill blood in what is, at bottom, a war of ideas.'[2] In this argument, religious belief becomes a proxy for imminent threat in order to justify wars of aggression. A self-proclaimed liberal advocates mass violence against a population defined by its religion, apparently violating the very liberal principles he claims to uphold.

How are we to explain this paradox? Are Maher and Harris bad liberals who fail to apply liberalism consistently? A better explanation is that they express contradictions at the heart of liberalism itself and stand squarely within a long tradition of advocating mass violence against racialised groups in the name of defending liberal values—a tradition that stretches from Napoleon to Tony Blair. Liberalism has long had a problem of only seeing the violence of racial others, while its own violence is hidden from view.

In the abstract, there is no reason why liberal principles of individual freedom cannot be applied consistently. And principled liberals have been essential to many struggles against racism and imperialism. But, liberalism is not just a body of ideas; it is also a social force. And, as such, there are structural reasons why liberalism keeps undermining its own ideals.

In his *Democracy in America*, Alexis de Tocqueville noted that the citizens of the liberal United States, 'each of them, living apart, is as a stranger to the fate of all the rest.'[3] The very individualism that has made liberalism a powerful force for freedom in some contexts also demands precisely this 'living apart'. Beyond a minimal shared commitment to the law, the bonds that connect people together in a liberal society are assumed to be a private matter emerging spontaneously through free association, not embedded in any deeper political connection. The liberal concept of tolerance emerges here: you are free to pursue your own cultural difference so long as it does not really make a difference by becoming political.

But liberal individualism is also the ideology of a social system—capitalism—that sustains itself through marginalising racial groups, through class exploitation, and through the drive to imperial expansion; thus the cultures of racialised groups and exploited classes are likely to become politically insurgent. The liberal demand to depoliticise culture, to abandon 'dangerous ideas', is then highly political and leads liberals to consider all manner of coercive initiatives to engineer the liberal subjects they feel are missing among oppressed groups. Liberalism then becomes a peculiarly cultural project that aims at upholding a 'way of life', if necessary through what Harris calls a 'war of ideas'—and he does not use the word 'war' metaphorically.

What this means is that the liberal principles that lead Maher to call for cannabis to be legalised (tolerate my choice to smoke what I like!) also lead him to Islamophobia (no tolerance for the intolerant!). It is also this same logic that has provided a rationale for colonialism for centuries and today shapes the perception of a 'Muslim problem'. It is the same logic that leads liberals to think that the appropriate response to police killings of black people is to say that we need to be more tolerant or better educated into liberal norms.

For liberals, if the system is producing social conflict, the problem is that some group of people is not liberal enough. But the system is the problem. Maher seems to think racism in the United States is a Republican Party problem or a southern states problem. If only.

Anti-racist politics is not a demand for liberal tolerance. It understands that having one's culture tolerated is very different from equal participation in shaping the future of society. Martin Luther King never called for tolerance; he called for racial equality and an end to poverty and war because he understood all three were intertwined products of the same system. A genuine fight against racial oppression requires the transcending of liberal forms of politics.

Notes

1. Dalia Mogahed and Ahmed Younis, "Religion Does Not Color Views about Violence," Washington, DC: Gallup, (September 9, 2011), http://www.gallup.com/poll/149369/religion-not-color-views-violence.aspx.
2. Sam Harris, *The End of Faith: Religion, Terror, and the Future of Reason* (New York: Norton, 2004).
3. Alexis de Tocqueville, *Democracy in America* (Ware, UK: Wordsworth Editions, 1998), 358.

36

Liberalism's Spawn: Imperialist
Feminism from the Nineteenth
Century to the War on Terror

Deepa Kumar

In a September 2014 interview with religion scholar Reza Aslan, CNN journalist Alisyn Camerota asked if Islam is inherently violent, given the 'primitive treatment in Muslim countries of women and other minorities.'[1] Aslan's response was that the conditions for women in Muslim majority countries vary. While women cannot drive in Saudi Arabia, in various other Muslim majority countries, women have been elected heads of state seven times. Before he could go on to say that the United States has yet to elect a woman as president, co-host Don Lemon interrupted, declaring: 'Be honest though, Reza, for the most part, it is not a free and open society for women in those states.'

This exchange captures the dominant perspective of the United States and European media regarding Islam. But where does this perspective come from? How is it that Lemon and others are so certain that women are treated 'primitively' in 'Muslim countries' that they feel they have the authority to call out a recognized scholar of religion like Aslan for intellectual dishonesty? Have they travelled extensively in Turkey, Indonesia, or Bangladesh, or read the scholarship on women's rights struggles in Morocco, Iran, and Egypt? How is it that Western commentators routinely and confidently make such proclamations about women and Islam, but offer no empirical evidence to support their claims and no acknowledgement of the great diversity of Muslim majority countries?

The answer lies in a ubiquitous, taken for granted ideological framework that has developed over two centuries in the West and is based on the appropriation of women's rights in the service of empire. Scholars such as Lila Abu-Lughod, Reina Lewis, Leila Ahmed, Marnia Lazreg, Rana Kabbani, Saba Mahmood, Lata Mani, and others have written extensively about what has variously been called 'colonial feminism', 'gendered Orientalism', and 'imperial feminism'. With its origins in the late eighteenth and nineteenth century context of European colonialism, this ideological framework rests on the construction of a barbaric misogynistic 'Muslim world' that must be civilized by a liberal, enlightened West—or as Gayatri Spivak famously put it, 'White men saving brown women from brown men.'[2]

In her recent book, *Do Muslim Women Need Saving?*, Abu-Lughod analyzes the more recent development of imperial feminism. She argues that the Afghan war gave rise to a new ubiquitous commonsense that sees militarism as the means to advance women's rights. In addition, the neoliberal era has given birth to a privatized means by which to address and appropriate gender oppression. A network of well-funded nongovernmental organizations (NGO), in collaboration with the United Nations and its various agencies, has produced what has been referred to as a 'neoliberal aid regime'. Inderpal Grewal and Victoria Bernal point out that in 2000, NGOs disbursed between twelve and fifteen billion dollars and that by 2012, the

NGO sector had become more powerful than the state in some parts of the world.[3]

NGOs, particularly those that receive large grants from corporate sources, have thus become the new missionaries. And by promoting neoliberal and imperial solutions to the problems that women face in the Global South, they have weakened both grass roots movements and national sovereignty.[4] Arundhati Roy notes that while NGOs in India have done good work, they have rejected a critique of neoliberalism. She argues that these heavily funded NGOs have enabled Western liberal feminism (the most funded brand of feminism) to define what feminism is, with the result that contemporary feminist analysis has been 'shorn of social, political and economic context.'[5]

Liberalism and Feminism

None of this should come as a surprise, given that liberalism as a philosophy and ideology developed in the context of the emergence of capitalism and various bourgeois revolutions. John Locke, considered the 'father of liberalism,' advanced notions of individual liberty and property that reflected the interests of the bourgeoisie. Liberalism is based on notions of individualism, equality of opportunity, and independence from state control. In its opposition to feudalism and absolutism, it asserted the autonomy of the individual. However, there were always exceptions and exclusions. Locke for example argued that the possession of private property gave men freedom and endowed them with a certain meritorious rationality, which by definition excluded women, the working class. Additionally, as a slave owner himself, Locke excluded slaves from his understanding of freedom and rationality.

Western feminism developed within the womb of liberalism.[6] In *A Vindication of the Rights of Woman* (1792), a formative text in the development of Western feminism, Mary Wollstonecraft sought to create a space for women within liberal rights discourse. She and various later feminists embraced the tenets of liberalism and individualism, but argued that women should also be granted rights on the grounds that they too are rational creatures. Wollstonecraft insisted that with access to education they would be able to attain rationality. Her focus, however, was primarily on middle-class white women. She was concerned that, as a result of industrial capitalism, they had lost their productive role in the household-based domestic economy. Thus, what animated early feminists was the goal of liberating middle-class women from their purported idleness and economic dependence.

While liberalism as a political doctrine represented a radical critique of feudalism and absolutism in the seventeenth and eighteenth centuries, it was, from the start, blind to questions of gender and race. Locke actively justified colonialism, arguing that English colonists were the 'chosen people' and that the natives of the New World were 'wild beasts'.[7] By the nineteenth century, liberalism became the ideological justification for slavery and colonization.[8]

As Uday Singh Mehta points out, various liberal and progressive thinkers such as John Stuart Mill, Jeremy Bentham, James Mill, and Thomas Macaulay championed liberal reforms at home. But in the colonies, they supported undemocratic and unrepresentative institutions on the grounds that the colonized were not sufficiently evolved to live in liberal democracies. In their writings on India, British liberals viewed the Indians as underdeveloped and child-like, and therefore in need of progressive parentage, which necessarily meant a denial of democratic rights.

Victorian feminism and the suffrage movement emerged in this context, and were thus marked by empire. Liberal middle-class feminists during this period adapted liberalism and argued for women's rights within Britain. For many, Britain could not be the 'great nation' it claimed to be, especially one dedicated to lifting up inferior races, if it continued to treat women as second-class citizens at home. Furthermore, the colony became a place where white middle and upper-class women could advance their status.

As Antoinette Burton points out, suffrage

> became necessary in the minds of many in order to take advantage of the pool of female personnel available for service in the empire, a pool that feminist agitation since the 1860s had helped to create and for the benefit of which the feminist press continually advertised colonial reform work. The plight of Indian women proved fertile ground for two principal causes undertaken by the British women's movement: women's employment opportunities and women's suffrage. Their advocates suggested that while the women's movement was crucial to the maintenance of the British Empire, empire was equally crucial to the realization of British feminists' aspirations and objectives.[9]

Imperial Feminism in the Twenty-First Century

The immediate context for a resurgence of imperialist feminism in the United States is the 2001 invasion of Afghanistan. Borrowing a trope from Britain in India and Egypt, and France in

Algeria, the United States argued that it was going to liberate Afghan women. Going against the wishes of Afghan feminist organizations that opposed US intervention, such as the Revolutionary Association of the Women of Afghanistan (RAWA), liberals and feminists in the United States linked arms with the Bush administration and supported the Afghan war.

In the Obama era, liberalism has become even more intertwined with empire. Despite substantial evidence to show that the US/NATO occupation had done little for women's rights, Amnesty International USA conducted a campaign in support of the continued occupation of Afghanistan. In 2012, advertisements depicting Afghan women in burkas appeared in public places, bearing the caption: 'NATO: Keep the Progress Going!' Amnesty also organized a summit that rearticulated imperialist feminist justifications for war, through the voices of such powerful women as Madeline Albright.[10]

What explains this tendency among liberals to continue to take positions contrary to the interests of Muslim women and women of colour, particularly given the forceful critiques by black and intersectional feminists of white middle-class liberal feminism? Among the numerous explanations, two are particularly noteworthy—racism and empire.

As noted above, a historical weakness of Western liberal feminism has been its racist patronizing of women of colour. It sees the latter less as allies and agents, than as victims in need of rescue or as instruments for advancing the careers of middle and upper-class women. This attitude prevails in relation both to women of colour within Western nation states, and to women in the Global South. It is what allows figures such as Madeline Albright and Hillary Clinton to pose as feminist saviors even while both, in their roles as Secretary of State, have advanced

US imperialism. The liberal conception of the state as a neutral body, rather than as a coercive apparatus used to advance capitalism and empire, lies at the root of such perspectives.

If imperial feminism has become the new commonsense in the twenty-first century, as Abu-Lughod argues, it is in no small part because liberalism itself is taken for granted. Rather than a particular ideology tied to capitalism, liberalism today is naturalized and universalized. Yet while liberalism and imperialist feminism operate as taken for granted ideologies, it is important to understand the role of propaganda in amplifying this world view.

The propaganda value of rescuing Muslim women has been seized upon by various institutions of the national security state. A WikiLeaks exposé of a CIA Red Cell propaganda memo shows the spy agency advising European governments on how to exploit the suffering of Afghan women in order to bolster flagging public support for the NATO occupation of Afghanistan.[11] It states that 'initiatives that create media opportunities for Afghan women to share their stories with French, German, and other European women could help to overcome pervasive skepticism among women in Western Europe.' This is not new. Colonialism has historically relied on native spokespersons and native collaborators to provide ideological cover for the colonial mission.

This is not to suggest that Afghan women who speak of the atrocities faced by the Taliban are automatically 'native informants' or collaborators with empire. Women have a right to speak out about their oppression no matter where they are located. However, there are those who either consciously or inadvertently enable empire. In *Brown Skin, White Masks,* Hamid Dabashi offers a trenchant critique of Ayaan Hirsi Ali, Azar

Nafisi, Irshad Manji, and others who peddle women's rights and gay rights as a cover for imperial intervention. In short, imperialist feminism does not emerge only from elites and their institutions in the West, but also from people in and from the Global South. Saadia Toor discusses new forms of imperialist feminism and outlines various actors, such as Gita Sahgal, who have reshaped this discourse in the current period and given it an even more grass-roots inflected liberal gloss.[12]

In the cultural sphere, TV shows such as *Homeland* reproduce imperialist feminism in its liberal guise. For instance, the publicity campaign for the fourth season featured an image of the female protagonist Carrie Mathison dressed in a red hood in the midst of a sea of women shrouded in black burkas. The women in black burkas presumably represent Pakistan, the country in which the season is set (as well as Islam and Muslim women more generally); whereas Mathison, with her red hood, blue gown, and white face represents the American nation. While Mathison is cast as the embodiment of liberal individualism, marked by her unique clothing and her active posture, the Muslim women are presented as indistinguishable, passive, and even threatening. The larger narrative is one of 'us and them,' highlighting the stark contrast between a society that values women and their agency, and a misogynistic and collectivist one that devalues women and blocks their individual liberation.

Consciously or not, it amounts to a repackaging of classic colonial Orientalist arguments about the civilized West and the barbaric East, but with the twist of a female protagonist. Thus, in place of the classic image of a nineteenth century British male assuming the imperial 'white man's burden' of bringing civilization to benighted savages, it is a liberated white American woman who has assumed that imperial burden and who, by turning around and looking at us, invites us to identify with her in this noble twenty-first-century cause. In the post-second-wave feminist era, feminism itself has been absorbed and appropriated into the making and remaking of imperial national identity.

Yet, it is not just white women who are the new protagonists of the twenty-first-century imperial feminist narrative. Occasionally brown women play this role, perhaps most prominently Hirsi Ali. However, other prominent brown and black women have also done so, particularly when they can serve as national symbols. One recent example is Maryam al-Mansouri, a UAE female pilot who received widespread media attention in the West.[13] Praised by liberals and conservatives in the United States (not withstanding one commentator's 'boobs on the ground' comment), al-Mansouri became a means to paper over the gulf monarchies' atrocious human rights record and to recreate the Arab nation. Even while the image of a Muslim female pilot served to disrupt the standard victim imagery, the larger narrative was one that cast the United States as savior leading a coalition of 'good Muslims' in a righteous war against ISIS. In place of T. E. Lawrence, we have Barack Obama.

Thus, while the protagonists in the twenty-first century imperial drama are black, brown, and often female, the underlying logic remains the same. As much as the narrative changes and appropriates the gains of various social movements, its principle thrust remains the reproduction of empire.

The vast majority of women in the imperial center do not benefit from empire despite the proclamations of liberal middle-class feminists. For instance, middle and upper-class feminists have routinely viewed women's participation in the military as positive. In 1991, after the first Gulf War, feminist

Naomi Wolf praised US female soldiers for eliciting 'respect and even fear' and for taking the struggle for women's rights forward. What she failed to mention is the over 200,000 Iraqis—men, women, and children—who were killed in that war. Similarly, while stumping for Hillary Clinton in 2016, Madeline Albright repeated her favorite slogan that there is a 'special place in hell for women who don't support other women'. What Albright did not repeat was her famous claim as Secretary of State that the deaths of half a million Iraqi children were an acceptable price of US and UN sanctions on that country.

Working-class women and women of colour in the United States cannot achieve their liberation on the bodies of the victims of empire any more than Arab women can by raining bombs on Syrians. Empire does not liberate; it subjugates.

Notes

1. "On CNN, Reza Aslan Explains How the Media Is Failing in Its Reporting on Islam," video televised by *CNN Tonight* on September 29, 2014, posted by Media Matters for America, accessed March 5, 2016, http://mediamatters.org/video/2014/09/29/on-cnn-reza-aslan-explains-how-the-media-is-fai/200942.
2. Gayatri Chakravorty Spivak, "Can the Subaltern Speak?," in *Marxism and the Interpretation of Culture*, eds. Cary Nelson and Lawrence Grossberg (Urbana: University of Illinois Press, 1988), 297.
3. Victoria Bernal and Inderpal Grewal eds., *Theorizing NGOs: States, Feminism, and Neoliberalism* (Durham, NC: Duke University Press, 2014).
4. Sangeeta Kamat, *Development Hegemony: NGOs and the State in India* (Oxford: Oxford University Press, 2002).
5. Sarah Shin, "Arundhati Roy: Feminism and Foundations, Burkas and Botox—An extract from Capitalism: A Ghost Story," Nov 19, 2014, accessed March 5, 2016, http://www.versobooks.com/blogs/1757-arundhati-roy-feminism-and-foundations-burkas-and-botox-an-extract-from-capitalism-a-ghost-story.
6. Zillah R. Eisenstein, *The Radical Future of Liberal Feminism* (Boston: Northeastern University Press, 1993).

7. Domenico Losurdo, *Liberalism: A Counter-History*, trans. Gregory Elliott (Verso, 2014).

8. Uday Singh Mehta, *Liberalism and Empire: A Study of Nineteenth Century British Liberal Thought* (Chicago: University of Chicago Press, 1999).

9. Antoinette Burton, *The Burdens of History: British Feminists, Indian Women and Imperial Culture, 1865–1915* (Chapel Hill: University of North Carolina Press, 1994), 11–12.

10. Saadia Toor, "Imperialist Feminism Redux," *Dialectical Anthropology* 36, no. 3 (2012): 147–60.

11. CIA Red Cell, "CIA Red Cell Special Memorandum; Afghanistan: Sustaining West European Support for the NATO-Led Mission-Why Counting on Apathy Might Not Be Enough," accessed March 5, 2016, https://mirror.wikileaks.info/leak/cia-afghanistan.pdf.

12. See Saadia Toor, "Imperialist Feminism Redux."

13. Ishaan Tharoor, "U.A.E.'s First Female Fighter Pilot Drops Bombs on the Islamic State," *Washington Post,* September 25, 2014, accessed March 5, 2016, https://www.washingtonpost.com/news/worldviews/wp/2014/09/25/u-a-e-s-first-female-fighter-pilot-dropped-bombs-on-the-islamic-state.

37

Who Exactly Is the 'We' That Liberalism Talks About?

Annabelle Sreberny

Two key terms of the liberal tradition, the 'people' and the 'public', are under siege.

The idea of 'we, the people' is enshrined in both the US and Indian Constitutions. But Richard Sennett once called 'we' a weasel word that insinuates itself into easy claims of identity.

The importance of the self-definition of a people begs the question of how a people is formed and how it is so acknowledged by others. Numerous theorists, including Étienne Balibar, Homi Bhabha, and Eric Hobsbawm have written about the narrative process needed to ground a nation, using a supposedly ready-made pre-history and set of cultural icons and myths. This 'we' is written backwards, not forwards, recuperating historical time and claiming an essential identity that actually has to be always reinvented. In such processes, minor differences sometimes become the basis of struggle for nation formation while other differences become minority positions with an other's whole.

But the political unit of the nation state is being challenged from two directions. It is challenged from the outside through the deterritorialisation of politics, the internationalisation of economies, the transnationalisation of the cultural realm, and other forms of practice and affiliation that erode sovereignty. But perhaps even more significantly, its cultural coherence is challenged from the inside, with the rising significance of minorities who manifest a range of different values, beliefs, and practices.

Time and again in the media debates in Britain around the Scottish referendum, the argument was made for a non-ethnicised version of nationhood at the same time that television speakers were introduced as having Scottish grandfathers or English forebears, an ethnicised version of a 'we'. Almost never was the issue of a multicultural nation with many 'peoples' in our midst raised. This speaks partly to the hostile anti-immigrant debate that is being so adeptly utilized by both UKIP and much of the tabloid press. But it also speaks to liberalism's difficulty to fully imagine a different form of the polity, a 'people' beyond the ethnicised nation state.

Arjun Appadurai argues that states and nations are each other's projects. There are some old nations/peoples—the Kurds, for example—still struggling for recognized statehood, while other states have to work hard to create a sense of nationhood; Qatar, for example. There remains a profound struggle on the international stage to ground and reground ethnicised political units. Indeed, the challenges to the 1915 Sykes–Picot map of the Middle East with the collapse of Iraq and Syria as coherent political units and with the proclamation of a Sunni caliphate by ISIS suggests the return of political units far larger than current nation states and based on competing definitions as to who 'we' are.

The issue of the constitution of difference remains central to contemporary politics *inside* states. Shlomo Sand, the Israeli historian, has renounced his Jewish identity as a way of spotlighting the privilege of Jewishness as the sole route to full citizenship in Israel, supposedly the only democracy in its region. Yet his personal choice hardly impacts on Israeli state practice that names him as a Jew in his passport, that ultimate arbiter of individual identity.

Beyond the issue of political rights lurks the question of cultural rights, the need for recognition of minority cultural beliefs and practices within the boundaries of nation states. If liberal democracies have moved someway toward de-ethnicisation, there remains more to be done. Scholars have noted the weakened nationalism of much history teaching in European schools and a general attenuation of ethnicised nationalism. But the problem is then shifted from the state's provision of an environment that welcomes minority cultures, however defined, to an individualized responsibility for tolerance and acceptance.

Notions of multicultural citizenship and cosmopolitanism raise important questions about our multiple affiliations in today's world. They do not resolve the feminist concern about women's rights being silenced by traditional group rights. And they do not settle the comparatively easy shift in rhetoric that can be made toward inclusiveness and diversity, without any structural processes of resource allocation nor a commitment to social justice. And yet, those tropes produced not only academic and intellectual but also public debate about the nature of liberal democracies, what stories they tell about themselves, who 'we' are, and how 'we' participate within them. David Cameron's insistence in early 2011 that multiculturalism had failed was made precisely in order to foster a stronger sense of national identity in order to prevent extremism, revealing a profound misunderstanding of almost all the issues at play.

If the idea of who constitutes the 'people' is confused, so too is the current idea of the 'public'. 'Public services' intended to benefit all, such as the National Health Service and the BBC, are underfunded and challenged by the rise of private providers of health care and media content. Yet the 'public school' system continues as a private bastion of privilege and still overproduces Westminster politicians, lawyers, and financiers. And even as more evidence reveals the full extent of social inequality in Britain, the 'public' is made to blame: 'we' are the illegal immigrants, scroungers, benefit fraudsters, couch potatoes. The victims of bank failure and financial mismanagement are blamed for the rise in the benefits budget, not those who finagle the system, cook the books, and refuse to alter weak tax regimes. A Tory welfare minister claimed that the rise of food banks was because 'people like a free meal' as he tried to bury a report documenting the real social need behind the growing phenomenon. And despite the plethora of reports that document the net economic benefit to Britain of immigrants (bracketing any other possible benefits) all the major political parties insist that the 'public' are very concerned about immigration, as if the 'public' does not include any immigrants. Increasingly, it is the excluded and the marginalized who are made to pay the price for incompetence, hubris, and hypocrisy, and the poor who are deemed at fault for their poverty. Using such linguistic sleights of hand, the Conservative government wishes to revive liberal notions of individual responsibility while avoiding those of the liberal, caring state.

The Scottish debate avoided discussion of the diversity of Britain and thus left many people out of the debate. We shouldn't let Cameron kill off multiculturalism, for all its challenges and difficulties. Nor can the Tory or UKIP definitions of the 'public' prevail; rather, we the 'public' can resist the destruction of our public services and institutions.

Now with Brexit, a little Englander mentality tries to revive a historic Great Britain that can stand alone, wilfully forgetting the huge range of international law and regulation to which all countries are subject, and finds no value in a greater multinational Europe that has brought warring countries and diverse linguistic communities into some kind of rapprochement and shared identity as Europeans. Indeed, the invocation of 'swarms' of migrants knocking on the doors of Europe only serves to reinforce the false but useful originary ethnic nationalism.

Echoing Alain Badiou, 'we, the people' has to be written forwards, in solidarity and political action and with a language rescued from illiberal politicians and their political spin doctors.

Notes on Contributors

Alejandro Abraham-Hamanoiel is a part-time lecturer at Middlesex University.

Patrick Ainley taught in secondary education before moving into further education. He is a researcher, reader, and professor in the School of Education at the University of Greenwich.

Abdullahi An-Na'im is Charles Howard Candler Professor of Law at Emory Law School. An internationally recognized scholar of Islam and human rights, and human rights in cross-cultural perspectives, Professor An-Na'im teaches courses in human rights, international law, and Islamic law. His research interests also include constitutionalism in Islamic and African countries, and Islam and politics. Before his current continuing project the *Future of Shari'a Blog*, he directed three major research projects that focus on advocacy strategies for reform through internal cultural transformation.

Michael Bailey teaches in the Sociology Department at Essex University. He is the co-author with Ben Clarke and John K. Walton, of *Understanding Richard Hoggart* (2011); and co-editor with Mary Eagleton, of *Richard Hoggart: Culture & Critique* (2011).

Haim Bresheeth is a film-maker, photographer, and a film studies scholar. He is co-author with Stuart Hood, of *Introducing the Holocaust* (2000); and co-editor with Nira Yuval-Davis, of *The Gulf War and the New World Order* (1991).

Başak Çalı is Professor of International Law at Hertie School of Governance, Berlin, and Director of the Center for Global Public Law, Koç University, Istanbul. She is author of *The Authority of International Law: Obedience, Respect and Rebuttal* (2015).

David Chandler is Professor of International Relations and Director of the Centre for the Study of Democracy, Department of Politics and International Relations, University of Westminster. He is the founding editor of the *Journal of Intervention and Statebuilding*; and editor of the new journal *Resilience: International Policies, Practices and Discourses*. His latest book is *Resilience: The Governance of Complexity* (2014).

William Davies is a Senior Lecturer at Goldsmiths, University of London and author of *The Limits of Neoliberalism: Authority, Sovereignty and the Logic of Competition* (2014), and *The Happiness Industry: How the Government and Big Business Sold Us Well-Being* (2015).

Costas Douzinas is Professor of Law and Founding Director of the Birkbeck Institute for the Humanities at Birkbeck, University of London. He is a regular contributor for *The Guardian* and author of *Philosophy and Resistance in the Crisis* (2013).

Natalie Fenton is a Professor in Media and Communications at Goldsmiths, University of London. She is Co-Director of the Goldsmiths Leverhulme Media Research Centre and Co-Director of Goldsmiths Centre for the Study of Global Media and Democracy. She has published widely on issues relating to news, journalism, civil society, radical politics, and new media and is particularly interested in rethinking understandings of public culture, the public sphere, and democracy. She is the author of *Digital, Political, Radical* (2016); co-author with James Curran and Des Freedman, of *Misunderstanding the Internet* (2016); and editor of *New Media, Old News: Journalism & Democracy in the Digital Age* (2010). She is on the Board of Directors of the campaign group Hacked Off and a founding member of the Media Reform Coalition.

Des Freedman is Professor of Media and Communications at Goldsmiths, University of London. He is the author of *The Contradictions of Media Power* (2014); and co-author with James Curran and Natalie Fenton, of *Misunderstanding the Internet* (2016).

Roberto Gargarella is Researcher at the Consejo Nacional de Investigaciones Cientificas y Tecnicas, Buenos Aires, and the Chr. Michelsen Institute, Norway. He is the author of *Latin American Constitutionalism (1810–2010): The Engine Room of the Constitution* (2013).

Priyamvada Gopal teaches in the Faculty of English at the University of Cambridge.

Jonathan Hardy is Professor in Media Studies at the University of East London and Secretary of the Campaign for Press and Broadcasting Freedom. He is the author of *Critical Political Economy of the Media: An Introduction* (2014).

John Holmwood is co-founder of the Campaign for the Public University and editor of *A Manifesto for the Public University* (2011). He is Professor of Sociology at the University of Nottingham and former president of the British Sociological Association.

Ratna Kapur is Global Professor of Law at Jindal Global Law School, Senior Faculty at the Institute of Global Law and Policy, Harvard Law School, and currently a Visiting Professor at Queen Mary University of London. She is the author of *Makeshift Migrants and Law: Gender, Belonging, and Postcolonial*

Anxieties (2010) and *Erotic Justice: Law and the New Politics of Postcolonialism* (2005). Her current book project is *Freedom in a Fishbowl: Gender, Alterity and Human Rights*.

Gholam Khiabany teaches in the Department of Media and Communications at Goldsmiths, University of London.

Ray Kiely is Professor of Politics at Queen Mary University of London. He is the author of *The BRICS, US 'Decline' and Global Transformations* (2015).

Monika Krause is an Assistant Professor of Sociology at the London School of Economics, and currently Fellow at the Helsinki Collegium for Advanced Studies. She is the author of *The Good Project: Humanitarian Relief NGOs and the Fragmentation of Reason* (2014), which examines the shared space of humanitarian relief organizations.

Deepa Kumar is Associate Professor of Media Studies at Rutgers University. She is the author of *Islamophobia and the Politics of Empire* (2012).

Arun Kundnani is the author of *The End of Tolerance: Racism in 21st Century Britain* (2007), and *The Muslims Are Coming! Islamophobia, Extremism, and the Domestic War on Terror* (2014). He teaches at New York University.

Colin Leys is an Emeritus Professor of Political Studies at Queen's University, Kingston, Canada, and an honorary research professor at Goldsmiths, University of London.

Howard Littler is an ex-president of Goldsmiths Students' Union and has since returned to his studies.

Kathleen Lynch is Professor of Equality Studies at University College Dublin and head of the School of Social Justice at University College Dublin. Her major area of equality research has been in education, but for the last ten years she has also been working on issues of egalitarian theory and practice with colleagues in Equality Studies. She is co-author with John Baker and Sara Cantillon, of *Equality: From Theory to Action* (2009); and the co-editor with John Baker and Maureen Lyons, of *Affective Equality: Love, Care and Injustice* (2009).

Robert W. McChesney is a Professor of Communication at the University of Illinois at Urbana-Champaign and co-editor of *Monthly Review*.

Nivedita Menon is a Professor at the Centre for Comparative Politics and Political Theory, Jawaharlal Nehru University, Delhi. She is the author of *Seeing like a Feminist* (2012) and *Recovering Subversion: Feminist Politics Beyond the Law* (2004).

Toby Miller is Emeritus Distinguished Professor at the University of California, Riverside, Sir Walter Murdoch Professor of Cultural Policy Studies at Murdoch University, and Professor of Journalism, Media and Cultural Studies at Cardiff University/ Prifysgol Caerdydd.

Kate Nash is Professor of Sociology, Co-Director of the Centre for the Study of Global Media and Democracy at Goldsmiths, University of London, and Faculty Fellow at the Center for Cultural Sociology, Yale University. She is author of *The Political Sociology of Human Rights* (2015).

Joan Pedro-Carañana is Assistant Professor of Media and Communication at Saint Louis University–Madrid Campus. His research focuses on the socio-historical transformations of communication, education, and culture. He is co-editor with Brian Michael Goss and Mary Rachel Gould, of *Talking Back to Globalization: Texts and Practices* (2016). Joan has also been active in a variety of social movements.

Julian Petley is Professor of Screen Media and Journalism in the Department of Social Sciences, Media, and Communications at Brunel University. He is chair of the Campaign for Press and Broadcasting Freedom, a member of the Board of Index on Censorship, and a member of the Advisory Board of Lord Puttnam's Enquiry in the *Future of Public Service Broadcasting*. He is co-editor with Robin Richardson, of *Pointing the Finger: Islam and Muslims in the British Media* (2011); and editor of *The Media and Public Shaming: Drawing the Boundaries of Disclosure* (2013).

Anne Phillips is the Graham Wallas Professor of Political Science at the London School of Economics, and is particularly known for her work in feminist political theory. She is the author of *Our Bodies, Whose Property?* (2013).

Jonathan Rosenhead is Emeritus Professor of Operational Research at the London School of Economics, and chair of the British Committee for the Universities of Palestine.

Annabelle Sreberny is Emeritus Professor of Global Media and Communication in the Centre for Media Studies at SOAS, University of London. She was the president of the International Association for Media and Communication Research from 2008–2012, and the first elected Director of the Centre for

Iranian Studies, SOAS, 2010–2011. She is the co-author with Ali Mohammadi, of *Small Media, Big Revolution* (1985), co-author with Gholam Khiabany, of *Blogistan: The Internet and Politics in Iran* (2010), and co-author with Massoumeh Torfeh, of *Cultural Revolution in Iran: Contemporary Popular Culture in the Islamic Republic* (2013). Her latest co-authored book with Massoumeh Torfeh, *Persian Service: The BBC and British Interests in Iran* (2014), examines the history of the BBC Persian Services as instruments of British public diplomacy and their entanglements in Irano-British politics. Her research interests include questions of diasporic community-building and identity-formation.

John Steel is a lecturer in the Department of Journalism Studies at the University of Sheffield. He is the author of *Journalism and Free Speech* (2012); and co-editor with Martin Conboy of *The Routledge Companion to British Media History* (2014).

Michael Wayne is a Professor in Screen Media at Brunel University. He is the author of *Red Kant: Aesthetics, Marxism and the Third Critique* (2014).

Milly Williamson is a Senior Lecturer in Screen Media at Brunel University. She is an executive member of the Media Communications and Cultural Studies Association (MeCCSA) and chairs MeCCSA's Women's Network.

Index